What business leaders and learning professionals have to say about *Lead with Your Customer*

"*Lead with Your Customer* is chock-full of real-world examples that give any leader much to think about and to apply. What really stands out in this book is the sense that excellent customer service can be good fun—as well as good business. The Six P's (Promise, People, Place, Process, Product, and Price) work in the public sector as well as the private sector."

—Camille Cates Barnett, Managing Director, City of Philadelphia

"World-class customer service is proven to be the cornerstone of great companies and brands. *Lead with Your Customer* has true application as a formula for success for any company that seeks to create a culture of high performance and consistent results through a leadership model that can utilize the Six Ps as its roadmap. To help build your world-class brand, I highly recommend this book for each member of your leadership team."

—Clint Westbrook, Regional Vice President, ARAMARK

"Mark David Jones and Jeff Kober have created a must-read for leaders in organizations from all sectors! *Lead with Your Customer* offers a simple and proven model to get your organization on the road to being best of class. Bursting with best-practice examples from 'real-world' companies, it offers a comprehensive framework and wisdom on how every business that cares about excellence can do the same. A wealth of ideas all in one place, this book could not be more practical—two thumbs up!"

—Shreyshree Raja, Director of Organizational Development,
Mount Sinai Hospital, Toronto, Canada

"Finally! A proven approach to business success from experts who have real-world experience. Every professional—public or private sector—needs these amazing insights. It's like getting a behind-the-scenes tour of the best companies—all in one extraordinary book. I'm recommending *Lead with Your Customer* to all our alumni around the world."

—Pamela Eyring, President, The Protocol School of Washington®

"Don't let terms like 'brand' fool you. *Lead with Your Customer* may be filled with private sector examples, but there is widespread application to the business of government. Focusing everyone on a vision, operationalizing your values, delivering on your promises, and understanding your employees and customers by walking in their shoes are powerful concepts. They apply to every federal, state, and local government; indeed, they are indispensable if you want to transform your bureaucracies."

—David Osborne, Co-author of *Reinventing Government*
and *The Price of Government*

"Whether you are an entrepreneur incubating thoughts of your next venture or you direct a global enterprise, *Lead with Your Customer* will help you combine time-tested truths with practical tools you can apply today. Let these world-class experts help you break away from mediocrity by challenging you and your organization's processes to attain world-class results!"

—Claudio Diaz, SPHR, Chief Human Capital Officer, Wipfli LLP

"In government, especially the Tax Collector's office, we don't think we have customers—how do you satisfy someone you're forcing to pay taxes? But we too have customers! Authors Jones and Kober provide powerful, compelling, and practical evidence that when leaders think of customers (both inside and outside your organization) first, and always, they will achieve extraordinary results."

—Martha Stark, former New York City's Finance Commissioner

"Too often corporate values are passed along as philosophies of business, but not linked to the reality of the corporate decision making. Yet, when organizations live their values as the foundation for all business decisions and systems, they create an organization of excellence. *Lead with Your Customer* is about more than creating customer service; it is about creating organizational excellence. This book provides a well-articulated roadmap for moving values from philosophy to reality, making the case that values are the essential business tool for sustained corporate success."

—David Cohen, author of bestselling *The Talent Edge* and *Inside the Box*, and
President of Strategic Action Group

"IT'S HERE! An all-in-one guide to building a successful customer-centered world-class business. This book speaks in terms of easy-to-implement tips, tools, and tactics that can be applied readily. *Lead with Your Customer* offers powerful insight and nearly instant return on your investment. This book has been transformational for our business!"

—Steve Riley, Head of Organizational Development,
Sidra Medical & Research Center, Qatar

"*Lead with Your Customer* erases the line between your external brand and your internal culture, and shows how they need to grow together as one organism. Happy customers, happy employees—you can't have one without the other."

—Ben Yazici, City Manager, Sammamish, WA

"Imagine! A book that helps you apply the Golden Rule to the most important people in your organization—your customers and the people who serve them. If you hold a fundamental belief in the dignity and capacity of people to contribute to a common purpose, *Lead with Your Customer* is for you. Incorporate these practical insights and easy-to-use techniques and watch the untapped energy in your organization produce world-class success!"

—Laurie Ohmann, CEO, The Public Strategies Group, Inc.

"*Lead with Your Customer* is essential reading for anyone in business. Especially in trying economic times, its values-based, logical approach can help any business keep focused on what is important, what leads to straight to the bottom line."

—Shelby Scarbrough, President, Practical Protocol
and Former Board President, The Entrepreneurs' Organization

"I was thrilled to see the message of culture, brand, and business results come together in one book. This is the first book that has done an effective job communicating the importance of creating an organizational culture that is consistent with the brand promise you want to deliver for your customer. *Lead with Your Customer* confirms that to sustainably maintain a WOW external customer experience, you have to invest and nurture a WOW internal customer experience—and the World Class Excellence Model provides a clear roadmap to get there."

—Tom Gavic, President, Performa Higher Education

"As a fan of efficiency, healthy relationships, effective leadership, and success, I am re-energized by the proven techniques shared in *Lead with Your Customer*. Consistent high performance does not happen by chance. Over 20 years in local government have taught me that we must make decisions that matter, and the 'blue print' for making the most profitable, defensible business decisions is only a purchase away in *Lead With Your Customer*. This book is simply a must-read for those of us who are serious about making an enduring impact on our careers and organizations."

—LaShon Ross, ACM/HR Director, City of Plano, Texas

"What huge value in a single volume! *Lead with Your Customer* is so rich with content that Jones and Kober could easily have spread the insight over a dozen books and each one would have been nourishing. One of their key insights is the understanding that keeping members of my team happy and keeping my customers happy are just different sides of the same coin. Since the same fundamental principles apply to both, I can apply a single approach to my internal customers and my external customers, and be wildly successful with each."

—Scott Farnsworth, President, SunBridge, Inc.

Lead with Your Customer

Transform Culture and Brand into World-Class Excellence

Mark David Jones

J. Jeff Kober

Foreword by Lee Cockerell

ASTD
PRESS

Alexandria, Virginia

ASTD Press is an internationally renowned source of insightful and practical information on workplace learning and performance topics, including training basics, evaluation and return-on-investment, instructional systems development, e-learning, leadership, and career development. Visit us at www.astd.org.

Ordering information: Books published by ASTD Press can be purchased by visiting ASTD's website at store.astd.org or by calling 800.628.2783 or 703.683.8100.

Library of Congress Control Number: 2009940016

ISBN-10: 1-56286-715-6
ISBN-13: 978-1-56286-715-7

The following are registered trademarks held by the authors: the Customer Compass, the Six Ps Customer Formula, World Class Benchmarking, and the World Class Excellence Model.

ASTD Press Editorial Staff:
Director: Adam Chesler
Manager, ASTD Press: Jacqueline Edlund-Braun
Senior Associate Editor: Tora Estep
Senior Associate Editor: Justin Brusino
Editorial Assistant: Victoria DeVaux
Inventory Coordinator: Eileen McKeown

Copyeditor: Alfred Imhoff
Indexer: April Michelle Davis
Proofreader: Kris Patenaude
Interior Design and Production: Kathleen Schaner
Cover Design: Ana Ilieva Foreman
Cover Art: iStockphoto, Frank Ramspott

Printed by United Book Press, Baltimore, Maryland, www.unitedbookpress.com.

Contents

Foreword

As the former executive vice president of operations for Walt Disney World, I often get asked to share Disney's secret to success. The short answer is the same for any world-class organization: "It's not the magic that makes it work; it's the way they work that makes it magic."

Lead with Your Customer by Jones and Kober provides a peek behind the scenes of Disney and many other world-class businesses—showing how they develop passionate employees, loyal customers, and superior business profits. While this book is full of actual examples from the world's most admired companies, the real star is the World-Class Excellence Model.

These days, there's a lot of empty talk when it comes to customer service. I've read hundreds of business books and spent years in the inner workings of some of the most respected companies of our time. This book is different. *Lead with Your Customer* shows both the strategic way the most successful companies expand their customer service to include their employees, as well as pragmatic tactics these companies use to achieve an industry-leading corporate culture and brand.

The approach shared in *Lead with Your Customer* is not a program, but a proven process of daily excellence and improvement. Throughout my career, I've personally seen the amazing results of following this approach. Becoming—and staying—world class isn't easy, but following the insights shared in these pages will make getting your best results much easier and more sustainable. You can spend the rest of your career falling short of your potential or you can lead with your customer. This book—and your customers—will show you the way to real world-class success.

The lessons from *Lead with Your Customer* apply to every professional in any kind of organization in any country who sincerely wants lasting results. I suggest you implement the tools in this book today—before your competition does!

Lee Cockerell
Former executive vice president of Walt Disney World
Author of best-selling book *Creating Magic*
www.LeeCockerell.com
March 2010

Preface

How do successful organizations consistently succeed? Their secret is simple, yet deep—they first seek to understand their customers' needs and expectations and then consistently deliver satisfying products and services. This book explains how your organization can emulate these excellent organizations by putting your customer first.

To make it possible to easily understand this customer-first approach, and thus enable you to transform your organization's internal culture and brand, we have created the comprehensive World Class Excellence Model. This model—the result of our decades of success as leaders at the Walt Disney Company and our years of experience and research working with many other large, midsize, and small successful organizations—can serve as a compass for leaders of all kinds of organizations, guiding their work toward bottom-line results, long-term success, and a world-class reputation.

Why This Book?

Why read another business book? This book will show you in a very practical way how to start with your customer and focus the right effort on the right things to achieve world-class results. *Lead with Your Customer* presents our leadership model through the lens of your customer—both internally, as you engage your employees (building your organization's culture), and externally, as you engage your customers (building your brand).

This book reveals the proven way to achieve excellent bottom-line results. Every day, some organizations achieve the best results in their particular industry—and not by accident. They work hard following and refining proven strategies and tactics that simply get better results than their competition.

There have been thousands of business books and articles about how to create an effective internal organizational culture. And there have been nearly as many books and articles about how to create a powerful external company brand. Experts have commented about how important these two issues are and how they are somehow interconnected, forming in effect two halves of a business puzzle, but no one has effectively joined them together—until this book, which integrates both in our new leadership model.

Throughout our years of experience with successful organizations of all sizes, we have observed striking behind-the-scenes similarities in how they have achieved consistently excellent results and earned the respect of both professionals and customers around the world. Eventually, we began to see a cohesive pattern and developed our new model, which reveals how these organizations transform their cultures and brands to become wildly successful and truly world class—and which likewise can enable you to optimize your own operation.

What do these legendary companies do that is different and better? Let's start with a quick analogy. Ask leaders if they are busy, and they will usually respond by saying that their "plate is full." Consequently, in today's fast-moving business environment, we're so busy day to day that any new responsibilities tend to "fall off the plate" when accountability begins to wane 6 to 12 months later—creating the infamous program-of-the-month problem.

How do successful organizations avoid the program-of-the-month trap when they make a change to improve their operations? Instead of making the change a discrete project, they do something radically different: They make it a sustainable, long-term process of improvement that isn't seen as an initiative with an end date. According to this approach, business issues—such as your values and vision, your methods of delivering service, and how you interact with people—should be constants, while everything else that is largely beyond your control—such as economic circumstances and political and social issues—shifts with the seasons. World-class companies establish a strategic foundation once and for all and then reinvest their savings of resources (the time, money, and effort not wasted chasing business fads) on adapting to the ever-changing context of business.

Obviously, no organization is perfect. Just because an organization is legendary today doesn't mean that it can't fail tomorrow. In this respect, we need to note one critical point: In this book, we're not providing hundreds of world-class business examples to have you focus on the particular organization being described; the future results of any organization will depend on whether it consistently executes the proven strategies we are exploring. Therefore, we ask that you instead focus on the strategy being exemplified and how it has been successfully implemented in the real world to achieve world-class results. These excellent results are only a natural outcome when an organization follows the proven principles of success—and this book shows how you too can learn to achieve these same results by focusing first on your customer.

How to Lead Your Customers to World-Class Excellence in the Real World

If you're looking for an academic book about business theories, this is not the one for you. Because this book is the result of our years of operational experience with numerous large, midsize, and small organizations all around the globe, our focus is resolutely on the real world. In fact, the book embraces a motto for which we've become known while working to make a difference with our clients: "If it doesn't work in the real world, you're wasting my time." The long-term, real-world success of excellent organizations is the result of their commitment to tenaciously follow tangible, pragmatic best practices. The book's primary purpose is to explain these benchmark practices in detail and illustrate how they are essentially followed by all best-in-class organizations.

Of course, everyone strives to be the best at what he or she does. What does "world class" mean in your particular industry? It's easy to think of high-end corporate legends like Ritz-Carlton, Tiffany's, and Mercedes as world class—but can smaller businesses also be considered world class? What about an industrial plant—can that type of operation be considered world class? Can government agencies or nonprofit organizations? And if so, how?

Many people mistakenly assume that "world class" can only refer to those brands that are the most expensive, the most luxurious, or even the most popular. Actually, the best of any particular class of operation in the world can legitimately be referred to as world class, but it seems that many want to claim that status without achieving the results that prove it.

After decades of working with hundreds of the most renowned organizations, we noticed a pattern among the most successful ones. The best in every class of operation profitably built the strongest brands by creating high-performing organizational cultures. This doesn't mean they're perfect—again, no organization is. Yet despite their imperfections, these diverse organizations excel in many ways—all worthy of benchmarking—and this book showcases their achievements.

The proven, real-life business tools presented here will enable you to achieve the same breakthrough results as so many other professionals have done—even in the most difficult situations. We encourage you to read this book, implement the solutions that work best for you, and begin realizing your fullest potential.

A Quick Preview

This book is organized in four parts. The four chapters in part I consider how you, as a leader, can establish the foundation for excellence. The six chapters in part II explore how to lead in forming the culture of your organization by optimally serving your employees. The six chapters in part III delve into how to lead in creating your brand by satisfying your customers with excellent experiences. And the four chapters in part IV describe how leaders can ensure alignment with their organization's core values and vision with integrity.

As you read these chapters, you'll learn how successful leaders have overcome the challenges you currently face. You'll discover how leading with your customer—including both external customers and internal customers (as you'll come to see your employees)—can transform your organization's results. And most important, you'll learn how to finally call a halt to the never-ending rotation of flawed improvement initiatives that, invariably, stop being effective. By implementing the proven approach of world-class organizations, you'll begin to realize the potential you've always envisioned. What comes next isn't just the first chapter of another new business book—it's the first step toward building lasting success for you and your organization. So let's begin our behind-the-scenes look at how legendary organizations lead with their customer.

Mark David Jones
J. Jeffrey Kober
March 2010

Acknowledgments

First and foremost, Jeff and Mark would like to thank our families, friends, and colleagues for the years of support during this project. We are grateful for you all. You inspire us to continue building a legacy of integrity and excellence.

In addition, we would like to acknowledge the many respected thought leaders, scholars, and pioneers of organization development who have come before us. Our efforts in this book to provide a unifying model of sustainable excellence build upon and synthesize the best of your valuable contributions.

Part I

Establishing the
Foundation for Excellence

Chapter 1

Your Customer Really Is the Key

What creates a successful organization? In our extensive work with a wide range of organizations in the private sector (including the hospitality, retail, health care, utilities, transportation, and food and beverage fields) and the public sector (at the federal, state, and local levels), along with companies based in dozens of countries, we have noticed two striking likenesses:

✦ All organizations are extremely similar in many ways.
✦ All organizations are completely unique in at least one way.

What do these similarities mean for your organization? They mean that not only do you have real opportunities to optimize your potential and make this your breakout year but also you're facing very real everyday business challenges that raise a number of questions—for example:

✦ How can we get anything important done when some leaders in my organization create obstacles?
✦ How do we create excellence when other decision makers keep slashing the budget?
✦ How can I make sense of my clueless or unreasonable customers?

+ Why do the same 20 percent seem to do 80 percent of the real work?
+ How do we deal with the poor attitudes around here?
+ What are we going to do to gain a competitive edge?
+ How do we get customers to comply with what we're asking them to do?

Although everyone has unique differences with regard to organizational culture and perhaps some proprietary technical expertise, your goals are the same as those of any other serious professional: to grow your business and to become as successful as possible.

Many excellent business books describe the strategic process that drives all organizational success. Whether it's the collected surveys of the Gallup Organization or the groundbreaking study featured in *The Loyalty Effect* by Frederick F. Reichheld (2001), the same pattern emerges. Simply said, this proven process is what makes a successful organization. In its simplest form, it looks like figure 1-1, which we call the Chain Reaction of Excellence Model. The model has four links, and each link is the catalyst for the next one—progressing from left to right in the figure. Here, however, let's consider these four links from right to left—to trace the path from the end result back to the beginning root cause.

Loyalty and Long-Term Success

To explain the Chain Reaction of Excellence Model, let's start with the box at the right side of figure 1-1: loyalty and long-term success. All organizations—in both the private and public sectors—are responsible for successful results, whether or not they generate revenue. Successful organizations generate value/profit, which they derive from loyal customers who return and even become advocates. With private businesses, there is the obvious

Figure 1-1. The Chain Reaction of Excellence Model

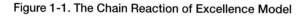

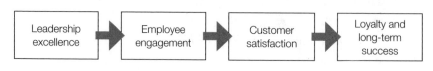

cause-and-effect process of generating revenue from goods and services. This applies to the public sector as well. Loyal constituents vote you back in, and happy citizens support you with the tax revenue and votes you need to fulfill your mission.

Customer Satisfaction

The next link in the Chain Reaction of Excellence Model shown in figure 1-1, moving from right to left, is customer satisfaction. The customers you serve externally are the reason you are in business—and stay in business. In public-sector and even some private-sector situations, we can also refer to these individuals as "compliers." Unless you understand what your customers want, you will not succeed. Actually, highly satisfied customers are vitally important, but mere satisfaction is not the goal. Truly engaged customers are the only customers who ultimately become loyal.

Employee Engagement

Continuing to move to the left, the next link in the Chain Reaction of Excellence Model is employee engagement. To transform your external results, you need to improve the key dynamics of this part of your operation, which drives these results. According to Jacob Schneid (2009) of the Canadian performance assessment firm the Momentum Group, "engagement has been referred to as an organization's ultimate competitive advantage—and possibly the only one it can fully control." When your employees are engaged, they are involved, committed, and passionate about accomplishing organizational goals. They typically function at more effective levels and provide excellent service and functional execution. World-class organizations view their employees as internal customers. Serving employees as customers, using the same tools utilized to engage external customers, can result in loyal employees—and all the benefits connected with this outcome.

Leadership Excellence

The next link in the Chain Reaction of Excellence Model shown in figure 1-1, moving to the left, is leadership excellence. Effective leaders throughout an organization are the catalysts for action, improvement, and excellence. Leaders who communicate a compelling vision, involve employees, and effectively manage company resources create the fertile environment within which employee excellence—and the rest of the Chain Reaction of Excellence—can be optimized to achieve long-term, sustainable success.

If you look at any successful organization, you'll find the four steps of the Chain Reaction of Excellence Model at work—and the results at any given step directly reflect the effectiveness of the previous step. Thus, if your organization is experiencing a problem in one area, the root of this problem can typically be found in the step that comes before it.

One important observation needs to be made here. At the heart of the Chain Reaction of Excellence Model—the middle two boxes of figure 1-1—are your employees and your customers. Consider what many do not: These two links of the model, representing these two basic categories of people, are what stand between you and the results you desire. There-fore, if you want to influence your organization's ultimate outcomes, you can only do so by influencing these people with whom you do business day by day. In this book, moreover, we explain how *both* categories of people are really your "customers"—your employees are your *internal customers,* and what are normally called simply your customers are your *external customers.*

Another insight is just as critical: You cannot achieve external cus-tomer loyalty without first achieving internal customer loyalty. When you model the attributes that create committed, passionate employees, you are laying the foundation for them to create relationships with their exter-nal customers that will result in repeat business, advocacy, and a bigger, better reputation. And you are also engaging employees who are more likely to become informal marketers to their family and friends—and even become loyal customers themselves.

Looking Ahead

Now that we have explored the Chain Reaction of Excellence Model, we can begin to see the truth that world-class organizations have discov-ered: Creating your organization's culture and building your brand are inextricably linked. The key to success and excellence is to serve both these types of customers with a seamless, strategic approach, which we will be modeling and exploring in the chapters to come. To accomplish this most logically, we've organized this book to mirror the Chain Reaction of Excellence. In the remaining three chapters of part I, we continue to explore leadership and the foundations for excellence, answering these kinds of questions:

+ What are the core, nonnegotiable aspects of my business?
+ How can I really understand my customers?
+ What types of leadership are most effective?
+ How can I understand how all the complex facets of business fit together?

In part II, we also explore how leading with your internal customers—your employees—creates your organizational culture. In this respect, legendary organizations keep in mind the following six priority questions that enable them to create the internal effectiveness and efficiencies that develop engaged employees and result in superior customer satisfaction:

+ How do you proclaim the promise of your culture?
+ How do you focus your employees on service behaviors?
+ How can you optimize the workplace?
+ How can you harness the power of processes?
+ How can you add value by investing in your employees?
+ How can you understand the value of getting the price right?

We devote a chapter of part II to answering each of these crucial questions about your culture, using many examples from renowned organizations, to show how these priorities fit together logically to achieve organizational excellence in relation to your employees.

In part III, we explore how leading with your external customers creates your brand and how the best organizations focus on the following six priority questions to engage, satisfy, and ultimately exceed the expectations of their customers:

+ How do you establish the promise of your brand?
+ How do you create an effective front line?

- How can you leverage the workplace to strengthen customer service?
- How can you create an impact through processes?
- How can you focus on products and services?
- How do you get the price right?

Again, as in part II, we devote a chapter to answering each of these crucial brand questions. And using more examples from world-class organizations, we show how these priorities fit together logically to achieve organizational excellence in relation to your customers.

Finally, in part IV, we explain how the most successful organizations put it all together to ensure alignment with their core values and vision, integrity, and results. In these final four chapters, you'll find the answers to these kinds of questions:

- How can I set the stage for successful transformation?
- What tools do world-class organizations use to anticipate customers' desires?
- How can I best provide service recovery when my customers aren't happy?
- How can I lead through the transformation process to achieve the best results?
- What can sustain outstanding results and strengthen my legacy as a leader?

As an organizing principle for the chapters making up the book's four parts, we introduce a groundbreaking, comprehensive operational model that enables us to progressively reveal the process of how to achieve excellent, sustainable results. First, however, we need to consider in more detail the hidden forces that drive the entire process of leading with both your external and internal customers in the quest to achieve world-class excellence.

Chapter 2

Leading with Your External and Internal Customers

The most important aspect of any organization is the people it serves—both external customers and internal customers (that is, its employees, as we've explained). Customers are like businesses; each one is unique, but they also have similarities that help us connect with them in meaningful ways. Compare any two organizations in the same field and you will often find two very different sets of customers. Though there are consumer patterns and trends, the best organizations are able to succeed by tailoring their products and services to each customer's real wants.

World-class organizations find ways to gather information about their customers that is relevant and meaningful. The most effective way to develop a balanced view of anything is to gather a representative variety of facts and figures—age, gender, income, purchase patterns, and the like—a mix of qualitative and quantitative data.

What do world-class organizations do differently and better? Along with collecting demographic information, they focus their primary efforts on gathering psychographic information, which helps them go beyond merely knowing about their customers to actually understanding them (as we explain just below).

One of the most elusive aspects of any business is the ability to genuinely connect with your customers. Every world-class organization has achieved consistent loyalty from its customers and employees because it makes the effort to understand them in a way the competition does not and uses those insights to build an experience that exceeds expectations.

Most people have had the experience of going to a store as a customer and being treated by an employee as "a wallet with legs"—feeling like the staff's only interest is in selling them something. In these kinds of situations, you feel you're only valued for your money. You get this impression because the employee is focused primarily on the transaction process rather than on you as a human being. The sales expert Jeffrey Gitomer actually has a trademarked tagline: "People don't like to be sold, but they love to buy." How true!

World-class employees are more interested in the interaction—with a focus on you as a person. Obviously, a customer strongly prefers being treated like a valued person, who happens to have money. Best-in-class companies still transact business and earn revenue (ironically, much more revenue than those that focus solely on the transaction), but they also get a relationship with an engaged customer—and the benefits that come with that effort.

You've probably heard the acronym "VIP," which is commonly defined as meaning "very important person." But to develop a more personalized kind of relationship, many benchmark companies have shifted the meaning of VIP to "very *individual* person." To succeed in the marketplace, world-class organizations realize that they must (1) understand their customers uniquely and completely, and (2) tailor their products and services to best fit the needs of their customers. In this age of mass customization, this reality cannot be emphasized enough. Thriving in your marketplace comes as a result of truly understanding what motivates your customers and why they buy. Paco Underhill, an expert on retailing and author of the best-selling book *Why We Buy,* explains it this way: "Even the plainest truths can get lost in all the details.... A phrase I find myself using over and over with clients is this: The obvious isn't always apparent" (Underhill 2000, 19).

Today, success requires the effective balance of sophisticated strategic thinking about the dynamics of your culture and brand and the tactical engagement of every employee in the quest to engage each and every unique customer on a personal, one-to-one level. This is what separates the experience customers might have with a world-class operation from an experience they might have with an average business.

To this end, we offer a psychographic tool for bridging the gap from just knowing about your customers to actually understanding them: the Customer Compass, shown in figure 2-1. If you think about a magnetic compass, it has four directional points—north, south, east, and west. Likewise, the Customer Compass also has four "directional" points, which can be studied both strategically and tactically to identify and respond to every customer's unique qualities:

- ✦ *Needs:* Beyond the most basic needs for food, water, and shelter, people express a variety of needs for products and services. Individuals have needs that are more relevant to them and are often hidden—but still drive their consumer purchasing decisions.
- ✦ *Expectations:* These are not about the perspectives and assumptions that you have of your customers. Instead, they target the preconceived notions that customers have of your industry, company, role, products, and services. Until you know what their expectations are, you cannot hope to exceed them.
- ✦ *Styles:* People respond to your products and services based on their individual styles or preferences. This point on the Compass includes four key styles that affect how the customer interprets and values the service experience.
- ✦ *Walk:* Perhaps the most powerful opportunity for understanding others is to "walk in their shoes." By considering the experiences of another person, you can learn how to direct your business choices toward what matters personally to that customer—and what, ultimately, results in a superior experience and a more profitable bottom line.

When everyone in an organization uses the Customer Compass to understand its customers and then consistently responds accordingly, a tremendous and special connection is created—with not only its external customers but also its internal customers (employees). To see how this works, let's look at each of the four points of figure 2-1 in more detail.

Figure 2-1. The Customer Compass

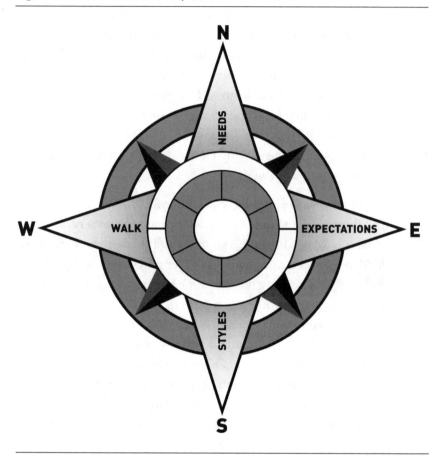

Needs

Finding true north allows any navigator to accurately travel in whatever direction he or she needs to go. North is the most critical and consistent of all directional points. The same could be said of the first point of the Customer Compass, N, for needs. Of all the four points, understanding customers' needs is the most important.

When referring to needs, we are not talking about the products or services for which customers are asking. These needs go much deeper than that—they're about what motivates them to want your product or service.

For example, at a pharmacy, the obvious reason a customer is there is to have a prescription filled. But consider the deeper question of "what are the circumstances surrounding the need for this prescription?" At a delivery service, transacting a letter-mailing process is simple, but the meaning behind that letter (a love letter? a late, important bill payment?) may add an entirely new dimension to the experience. By considering these personally relevant aspects, anyone can do a better job of connecting with and serving a customer.

Certain common elements of the human condition span culture, race, gender, and any other method used to categorize the people of this world. The unified category of "human being" is a common denominator that can provide universally valuable insights. In the pursuit of better understanding human nature, experts from all fields of study have conducted research about people throughout history. In an effort to bring together the key findings from these previous investigations, we have assembled a targeted list of humanity's strongest and most fundamental motivators. Pondering these universal needs is the first step in really understanding your customers. They include

1. the need to be heard and be understood
2. the need to belong and contribute
3. the need to feel stable and in control
4. the need to feel significant and special
5. the need to be successful and reach one's potential.

The goal is to consider these five needs so that you can learn to better understand your customers (both external and internal) and leverage this awareness to more personally serve them and exceed their expectations. Let's examine each need in more detail.

The Need to Be Heard and Be Understood

The first of the essential customer needs is an umbrella concept that encompasses all the others. To provide great service to your customers, you must first understand them. A vital component to connecting with another individual is communicating in a meaningful way.

If we don't understand each other, we probably won't comprehend how the remaining real needs apply. Well-meaning organizations often develop services and products for their customers that are not well received simply because the customers feel that the company doesn't care enough to make the effort to hear and understand them.

Successful companies have discovered that the most effective approach is to first focus on others. This concept is explained very well in *The 7 Habits of Highly Effective People,* by Stephen R. Covey (1989), where habit number five is "Seek first to understand and then to be understood."

Coming to have a true understanding of another person means more than gaining a thorough knowledge of facts about his or her concerns. In fact, this is the common misunderstanding of most people—in both their personal and professional lives, because it's human nature to stop really listening to someone once we assume we've understand their key points. Even if you're correct in understanding the content of a conversation, you haven't always paid close attention to the other crucial dimensions of the communication—enabling the other person to *feel* heard and understood. This involves empathy, feeling with the other person, so that you're paying attention to the associated emotions involved with that person and the topic you're discussing. This doesn't mean you have to cry along with the person or act angry if he or she is behaving angrily. But it does mean that you must engage individuals long enough until they *feel* as if they have been heard. This requires more than an occasional nod in agreement or "parroting back" what they have just said. Helping someone feel heard requires making the effort to ask open-ended questions, look for examples, and align your emotional response with what is really being said—even "between the lines."

Amazing things happen when people feel that you really hear and understand them. Emotional walls come down, and healthy relationships bloom. By attending to this human need, you set the stage for trust, engagement, and long-term loyalty—the "holy grail" of every organizational operation. Shelby Scarbrough, past board president of the internationally acclaimed Entrepreneurs Organization, suggests that successful organizations focus on deep understanding: "Healthy (work, client, employer/employee) relationships that begin with courtesy and end with mutual respect and trust are deep and lasting and loyal" (Scarbrough 2009).

The Need to Belong and Contribute

As the American Express slogan states: "Membership has its privileges." Another fundamental human need is belonging and having an opportunity to contribute in a meaningful way.

Human beings are social creatures. Throughout recorded history, people have gravitated toward living in groups. Friendships, families, communities, and even national pride are reflections of our common need to belong. It's easy to observe everyday behaviors that reflect this innate need:

- Teenagers purchasing high-end shoes from Nike or dressing in the latest styles from Abercrombie & Fitch.
- Cheering not for the team most likely to win but your hometown team, whether it's a small-town team like that of the local high school or a big-city team like the NBA's Orlando Magic.
- Choosing to be among the "cool" people who buy Apple products or choosing to purchase the more popular Microsoft personal computer products. This is currently seen in the workplace competition between the BlackBerry and Apple's iPhone.
- Voting along Democratic, Republican, or even independent lines because you find yourself in alignment with a given political party—or a long-held family tradition.
- Choosing sides in the cola wars between Coca-Cola and Pepsi.
- Insisting that others "buy American" by purchasing only Ford, Chrysler, or GM cars and trucks.
- Joining social organizations such as the Rotary and Kiwanis clubs—or online social networks like Facebook and LinkedIn.

Pop culture in general is a manifestation of our individual need to feel a part of a greater whole and to contribute to it. Even individuals who hate going along with the crowd often do so, knowing that they will join with others who resist the same. For instance, Virgin and Harley-Davidson have built their brands by targeting those who want to stay in touch with their antiestablishment yearnings.

Feeling as if they belong and are contributing gives people the courage to do things they might not do on their own. Conversely, it may cause them to behave in foolish ways that they would have never considered on their own. Understanding individuals' need to belong and contribute gives us a perspective from which to better address their wishes through the products and services we offer.

The Need to Feel Stable and in Control

When observing how people react in difficult times, such as during the recent global economic instabilities, it is easy to understand how much people value feeling stable and in control of their circumstances. Providing much-desired stability as part of a professional business relationship can be accomplished in many different ways. Consider the following:

- ✦ The motto "You're in good hands with Allstate" is really about using an insurance policy as a tool for obtaining peace of mind.
- ✦ Old bank buildings for institutions such as Bank of America and JP Morgan were formidable structures constructed of stone and large columns to suggest a solid, stable structure that would protect your money.
- ✦ For many years, the Walmart tagline was "Always low prices." This assurance communicated confidence that you could shop and still control your budget.
- ✦ Being able to select from among a range of 31 ice cream flavors made Baskin-Robbins a favorite among consumers who wanted more choices.
- ✦ "Have it your way" was one of the most successful ad campaigns used by restaurant giant Burger King—because people wanted control and choice about their meal, despite quick service limitations.

Entering the portals of Disneyland, you pass under this inscribed quotation: "Here you leave today and enter the world of yesterday, tomorrow, and fantasy." The appeal in a Disney theme park is that you're leaving the uncertainties of the real world and entering a beautiful, friendly environment. It's safe. Aware of this human need, the Walt Disney Company's Imagineers (that is, its artists and engineers) purposefully create buildings on a scale so their upper floors decrease in size. Rather than being dwarfed by imposing buildings, as one would experience in a crowded city, Disney adjusts elements of the experience to enhance its guests' (customers') sense of control and stability.

After the terrorist attacks of September 11, 2001, a more prominent security presence was positioned at the front of the Disney theme parks to check bags. Surveying its guests' perceptions, Disney found that they actually liked the feeling of enhanced security that came with knowing everyone's belongings were being checked to ensure their safety. The simple actions of checking bags communicated something far more important in the minds of Disney's customers; Disney understood their concerns, and it was dedicated to taking the extra steps so they would feel stable and secure—a commitment even more important during uncertain times.

In short, Disney succeeds because it builds credibility and trust—so much so that its guests are comfortable "handing over their control" because they're confident that it is capable of controlling everything for them, with their best interests at heart. And when a company has earned this kind of customer loyalty, along with becoming a wonderful advocate, it's secured many long-term sources of very profitable revenue. (For more on Disney's successful development, see Thomas 1998.)

The Need to Feel Significant and Special

Another fundamental human need is to feel as if we matter. People like to feel unique and special. What are some ways in which world-class companies accomplish this? When you review all the variables, it all comes down to taking time and making an effort. Here are just a few examples:

- ✦ Taking additional time to hear someone's concern, which is connected to the first need described earlier—feeling heard and understood.
- ✦ Recognizing the specific accomplishments that a person has made.
- ✦ Arranging for exceptions to policies and procedures to take care of higher-priority individual needs.
- ✦ Rewarding an individual's contribution in a way that's meaningful to him or her.

+ Sacrificing your will or opinion on a particular matter for the benefit of another person.
+ Doing something special for yourself.

In doing these types of things, it is important to keep in mind the difference between the Golden Rule and the Platinum Rule. The Golden Rule is about treating others the way you would want to be treated. But the most successful companies abide by the more effective Platinum Rule: Treat people in a way *they* want to be treated.

The Need to Feel Successful and Reach One's Potential

Why is it important to understand people's need to experience growth and development? How can you help others reach their fullest potential? It is human nature to want to succeed. With today's relentless pressure to achieve, the thought of not living up to your potential can become frustrating, and even paralyzing.

What factors support someone in reaching his or her potential? Consider these:

+ Having the courage to try new things.
+ Being dissatisfied with the status quo.
+ Enjoying the rush that comes with achieving goals.

Conversely, what are obstacles to someone reaching his or her potential? Consider these:

+ Undermining circumstances.
+ Having previously experienced defeat.
+ Being naive.
+ Having a limiting attitude about possibilities.
+ The perceived risk of blame, disappointment, or other negative consequences.
+ A lack of support or encouragement.

We all have the responsibility to help people reach their potential, including our own. World-class organizations strive to optimize every person's ability to leverage every opportunity—every day.

The Essential Customer Needs—Summing Up

The degree to which an organization succeeds in understanding and meeting these essential customer needs is the degree to which it succeeds in fulfilling its purpose. On those occasions when an organization has failed to meet your expectations, it's because it has failed to pay attention to one or more of these five needs. This can be true of any company or organization—whether it's a hospital, bank, or retail store. Creating a great customer experience is about more than providing products and services. It's about addressing the real needs of the people you serve. You simply must understand your customers to grasp what they really need.

Expectations

The second Customer Compass point is E, for expectations. Typically, when referring to customer expectations, the concern is about organizations' perspectives on and stereotypes about their customers. But world-class businesses take a completely different view of this issue. This real need focuses on the preconceived notions that customers have of *you*—your industry, your company, your role, and even you as an individual. Customers have differing expectations about different industries and businesses. For example, consider these sample experiences:

+ Purchasing a time-share.
+ Acquiring a used car.
+ Being sold a product or service by telemarketers.
+ Going on rides at a traveling carnival.

Generally speaking, the public's expectations of these experiences tend to be negative—even when a person hasn't personally done it. Now consider the expectations you might have of these sample experiences:

+ Attending Yale or Harvard.
+ Purchasing a Mercedes-Benz.
+ Shopping at Tiffany's.
+ Staying at a Ritz-Carlton.

Though some might have a negative expectation about the costs of these experiences with elite products and services, polls usually show positive connotations for them.

In this vein, try an imaginary exercise: Suppose for a moment that you arrive at a beautiful Ritz-Carlton hotel. No one appears at the front desk, so you ring the bell. Out comes an employee in a wrinkled, dirty suit, smoking a cigarette. "Whadya want?" he mumbles. You inquire about checking in. He responds with "Hold your horses, can't you see I'm on the phone?" After loudly continuing his phone conversation about placing a bet on the next horse race, he turns to you and tries to sell you a more expensive room you didn't reserve.

Would you expect this experience to actually occur at a Ritz-Carlton? Probably not. It's completely out of alignment with their motto of "Ladies and Gentlemen serving Ladies and Gentlemen." Unfortunately, however, this type of negative experience is probably more associated with the stereotypical process of purchasing a used car. As painful as it is for sellers of used cars to hear, when people are surveyed to describe the typical experience of buying a used car, the vast majority share a story about "a group of men lined up outside the dealership, dressed in plaid suits, smoking cigarettes, readying themselves to swoop down on you like a vulture and sell you a lemon."

There is one key thing to understanding your customers' expectations: You can't exceed their expectations until you really know what they are. This is why CarMax stands out so much from typical expectations about buying a used car. CarMax considered all the stereotypical negative expectations about its industry and then did the opposite, leveraging them to its advantage. Its showrooms are clean, bright, and spacious. It has an enormous selection of vehicles, which go through a 100-point inspection process to ensure that they aren't lemons. And its efforts to reverse expectations based on stereotypes also extend to its sales staff. They don't haggle over price with you. In fact, the final price is clearly displayed on each car, and you can either accept it or not. Overall, the CarMax buying process is designed to be hassle free, supportive, and simple. The staff is largely there to help you with information about each car and assist you with test driving the cars of your choice.

CarMax doesn't even refer to itself as used car dealership. It talks about previously owned vehicles. It targets every negative issue evoked by the thought of "used car sales" with the intent of creating a positive alternative. Thus, even if you are considered part of a stereotypically bad industry, when you position yourself as clearly different from these kinds of expectations and instead deliver an exceptionally satisfying customer experience, you will set your organization apart from the competition.

Organizations can become incredibly successful when they really seek to understand the expectations of their potential customers and then use them to their competitive advantage. For another example, consider the experience that might come to mind when it comes to buying a time-share. The Disney Vacation Club understood these perceptions—again stereotypically negative—and viewed them as an opportunity to change an entire industry.

However, Disney's choice to enter the time-share industry did not come quickly or easily. The reputation of the time-share industry closely mirrored that of used car sales—complete with the very low regard that comes with that experience. So rather than using the tainted term "time-share," Disney created the phrase "vacation ownership" to take the focus away from the real estate product and focus more on the customer's vacation experience—the real reason most families choose to invest in a time-share (the "ownership" concept meets one of the essential customer needs—to be stable and in control). Table 2-1 shows the differences between the typical time-share approach to business (and results) and Disney's approach.

Understanding the expectations of others and leveraging them for your—and your customers'—benefit can be a powerful way to follow the Customer Compass. It's an essential ingredient that separates struggling companies from consistently thriving companies.

This same principle applies to your employees, your internal customers. Often someone's choice to work in a particular trade or even for a specific organization has much to do with his or her expectations of those types organizations. Many times, their expectations were first shaped as customers—"It was a fun place to visit; I thought it would be a fun place to work." In truth, one of the biggest organizational challenges is dealing with

Table 2-1. The Differences Between the Typical Time-Share Approach and the Disney Approach

Time-Share Industry Approach	Disney Vacation Club Approach
Real estate investment—you are buying a piece of property	Points investment—you are buying access to a wide range of properties.
Limited to particular week, location— use or lose each year	Complete flexibility about date, location, and accommodations
Focus: the transaction (sell to customer)	Focus: the interaction (help customer buy)
Bonus on sales and margins	Bonus on satisfaction and sales
Given 3 days before contract becomes binding; 10 percent "opt out"	Given 30 days before contract becomes binding; less than 1 percent opt out
Salesperson's role/responsibility ends with sale	Salesperson continues to answer questions/ support customer after sale
No interaction between Sales and Operations or Marketing	Weekly meetings/newsletters between Sales, Operations, and Marketing
5 percent repeat purchasers	65 percent or more repeat purchasers
15 percent referrals (industry average)	80 percent or more referrals

employees who have been disappointed with the experience of working for an organization that hasn't been as tremendous for them as was the earlier experience of being its external customer. They often leave the organization feeling frustrated and disillusioned by it, especially if they grew up dreaming of working there.

Styles

The third Customer Compass point is S, for styles. This refers to the individual and personal styles of how people respond to life around them. Recognizing that human beings are wonderfully diverse, it is helpful to identify the critically different styles in which people think and behave, and then adapt your products and services to their preferences. Pam Eyring (2009), president of the renowned Protocol School of Washington, comments on the importance of dealing effectively with differences of style in the workplace: "International protocol, etiquette, and image involve a wide range of things, but at their foundation, they are about social intelligence. We are always a reflection of our company—and even our country. Success in any interaction requires a real understanding of ourselves and others, and the ability to take the appropriate action to achieve the best results—from the perspective of our guests."

To assess people's individual and personal styles, there are numerous psychological instruments and personal inventories on the market today. The social styles assessment is among the most respected and the easiest to apply in a pragmatic organizational environment. In this regard, Roger Reid and David Merrill (1981) developed an assessment instrument showcasing four social styles of individuals—analytical, driving, expressive, and amiable—that can be particularly useful for understanding the compass styles point. These four styles are based on two factors: assertiveness, the effort a person makes to influence the thinking and action of others; and responsiveness, the extent to which a person reacts readily to influence or stimulation by displaying his or her feelings. Knowing the four social styles helps us understand others and their Customer Compass. Let's briefly consider each one.

Analytical Individuals

Analytical individuals tend to be serious and exacting. They tend to follow a more logical path to produce understanding. They prefer to take time to think before declaring that they are right, but once they have declared their "rightness" in the matter, they are adamant based on their very thorough analysis. Those who are analytical tend to focus on data and other sources that require less personal interaction. Analytical types may appear overly cautious. As a result, others may view analytical people as being indecisive.

Driving Individuals

Individuals with a driving style focus more on telling and less on asking. This reflects their ability to easily interact with others, their energy to share ideas, and the passion with which they take on projects. Driving individuals tend to be independent, formal, practical, and dominating. They seek to make things happen—and they do so by initiating action. They usually do better when they take the time to listen more carefully. When working with others to complete a task, they see themselves taking the lead simply for the purpose of getting matters moving. If necessary, they may choose to do it themselves, rather than waiting for others to get involved. If driving types are not careful, they can "burn bridges" to their colleagues.

Expressive Individuals

Expressive individuals gravitate toward interacting with others. They tend to be animated and impulsive. Though they can be seen as forceful, opinionated, and persuasive, they are usually less controlling. The decisions of some expressive people can be based on gut feelings without much outside validation. On one hand, this sort of behavior can get others to cooperate with them, because their expressiveness is inspiring. On the other hand, they will find it difficult to tolerate situations where there is little positive response or overt recognition. When expressive types are unhappy, they can often be your most outspoken critics.

Amiable Individuals

A clear strength of amiable people is that they tend to be very friendly. They also prefer to be pliable, dependable, supportive, and open. Amiable types are more focused on asking others than telling others. They also tend to be more emotive and less controlling. They value harmony and are careful not to disrupt the dynamics of the group. In terms of getting the job done, they do well in a cooperative setting. And if tension emerges, they prefer to deal with that problem and the feelings of others rather than moving on and ignoring them. They may have difficulty acting independently or in taking a personal stand when the job demands it. Because amiable types are sensitive to the needs of others, they can help to pull a team together.

Caveats on Styles

No one style accurately reflects the entire personality of an individual, but everyone tends to gravitate toward one style more than another. Our observation is that, based on numerous formal and informal surveys over the years, each of the four style types described here will make up about 25 percent of an organization's staff—particularly in larger, more successful organizations. It appears that higher levels of diversity could possibly contribute to an organization being a more capable provider of superior results. Consider these observations about how style differences affect world-class service:

+ You have key strengths that are valuable.
+ Your team members offer different strengths than you do.
+ You are able to understand customers with styles like yours better than those whose styles differ.
+ Consider that about 75 percent of those with whom you interact have a different style than yours.
+ "A strength overdone becomes a weakness"—for example, confidence is a strength until it evolves into arrogance; then it becomes a weakness. Be certain that your strength is leveraged appropriately to the situation and complements the styles of those with whom you are interacting.
+ Great leaders are adaptable to other styles, regardless of their own personal preferences.

Understanding the styles of others is fundamental in seeking to provide products and services that surpass those of the competition. It also will give you direction in creating a high-performing culture. There is power in understanding the styles of your customers, and in incorporating the styles of your employees in addressing customers' needs.

Walk

The fourth point of the Customer Compass—W, for walk—focuses on a critical commitment that every world-class organization must demonstrate, at both the macro and micro levels. Here, "walk" means figuratively walking in the shoes of your customers—whether they are external customers or internal customers (employees).

According to Kim Tudor (2009), director of the Barbados National Initiative for Service Excellence, "there is a need for all levels of employees—including the CEO—to go through the process that the customer experiences from start to finish at least twice a year. This firsthand experience, coupled with ongoing feedback from customers, will help in truly understanding the customer."

World-class organizations are renowned for their practice of experiencing their products and services from the customer's perspective. For example, J. Willard Marriott, the patriarch of the Marriott family, learned about the customer's perspective by managing as he walked around and explored. When he spotted a small, successful A&W root beer stand in Salt Lake City, he knew that it would be a success in Washington because he had lived there and knew how miserably hot its summers were. As the autumn leaves began to fall, he was reminded how bitterly cold the winter got in that area, so he quickly adapted to meet customer demand by opening a Hot Shoppe, which sold not only root beer but also tamales and chili—and became the foundation for what would become one of the largest restaurant chains in the eastern United States, A&W. And the lessons it taught would become the foundation for one of the world's most successful hotel and hospitality service chains, Marriott.

In explaining J. Willard's practice of managing by walking around, his son, Richard, said the following:

> You cannot run a service business without walking around and seeing what's going on in the operation. You can't be in the office looking at the books all day and know what's really happening with your customers. My father would go out and talk to the customers, talk to the employees, and inspect the units. He believed that you can't expect what you don't inspect. If you ask somebody to do something and never go back to check and see if it's done, it might get done the first time, but it probably won't get done thereafter. You've got to get out there, check and make sure your associates follow through on their commitments, and let them know you will be checking. Then you must show appreciation to people for doing a good job. If they're not doing a good job, explain how to do the job properly and give them encouragement. (Marriott 2003, 7)

What are some additional ways that you can walk in the shoes of your customers? At the high-end architecture, interior/landscape design, and construction group Anthony Wilder Design/Build Inc., everyone in the 30-member office visits active job sites to witness how their extended team creates new homes for their clients. New executives at Starbucks who haven't worked their way up the ranks can work as front-line baristas for months before assuming their new role with the company. Everyone at the head office of Pret Star spends time in the stores making sandwiches for customers every quarter.

Summing Up

Using the Customer Compass (figure 2-1) is not just an exercise or employee activity. It's really about consistently being aware of the mindset of your customers—both internally, of your employees, and externally, of the people whom you serve—and understanding them so totally that your actions are in alignment with what they really want. When the compass is used consistently, world-class companies find that it becomes almost intuitive. The compass can help you keep these things in mind; and in upcoming chapters, we'll see how the Customer Compass completes our overall model for achieving excellence in satisfying customers.

World-class organizations understand that it's not the customer's job to articulate what will exceed his or her expectations—it's the organization's job to deliver the product or service that will exceed customers' expectations. People don't always know what they want until they see it. This explains what Henry Ford meant years ago when he stated: "If I asked people what they wanted, they would have asked for a better horse." At Apple, Steve Jobs feels the same way. As he recently put it, "Customers don't know what they want; we have to tell them what to buy."

Is this arrogance? Perhaps a bit, but it's been justly earned after one has invested a lifetime in understanding what people really want in a particular field. When you work to understand your customers and honestly want them to have every need fulfilled and have every expectation exceeded, you will have earned the right to be that trusted adviser who guides their buying decisions. Apple and Ford succeeded because of the intuition that develops from really understanding the customer—of practically becoming the customer themselves. The first step is choosing to walk, each and every day, in the customer's shoes.

Next steps for understanding how to lead using the
Customer Compass:

◆ What needs do your external customers have? What needs do
your internal customers (employees) have? What are your
needs?

◆ What are your customers' expectations of your business or
organization? What are your employees' expectations of your
business or organization? What are your expectations?

◆ In which style do you typically operate? How can you use that
style as a strength? How can you keep that strength from
becoming a weakness?

◆ How do you walk in the shoes of your customers and
employees?

Chapter 3

Achieving Proven Leadership Excellence

What is leadership excellence? Think of the name of someone you regard highly as a leader. It might be someone for whom you work. It might be someone famous, a historical figure, or someone from your old neighborhood.

Now consider what makes this leader so great in your opinion. Identify the qualities that are strongest in this individual, such as:

+ Communicating a compelling vision.
+ Acting with integrity.
+ Listening intently to others.
+ Being honest at all times.
+ Serving rather than managing.
+ Involving others.
+ Holding himself or herself—and others—accountable.
+ Focusing on what's important rather than what's urgent.
+ Inspiring others to go the extra mile.
+ Taking time to support those who need it.

These are just sample qualities; your criteria may also include other qualities. There are thousands of business books about leadership. When analyzing the most successful leaders of world-class organizations, the two general things they all have in common are a high degree of integrity and caring enough about people to accomplish important things—despite the risk.

The true measure of a leader is taken by his or her followers. As an aphorism states, "A leader without followers is just someone out taking a walk." The bottom-line connector between a leader and his or her followers is their values. People will not passionately follow any leader who does not share their core priorities. We will go much more in depth about these core drivers in discussing the World Class Excellence Model in chapter 4.

Leaders and Managers

Let's set the record straight about the terms "leader" and "manager." In recent years, there have been many attempts to create a false dichotomy between these terms. You may have seen some comparisons, such as the ones shown in table 3-1. These kinds of comparisons can give the impression that the role of "manager" is a "bad" function but that of a "leader" is a "good" one. This is woefully inaccurate. In truth, two points must be made here.

Table 3-1. Examples of Comparisons Creating a False Dichotomy between Managers and Leaders

Manager	Leader
Enforces consistency	Elicits creativity
Duplicates	Originates
Evolves	Revolutionizes
Asks how/seeks methods	Wonders why/seeks motives
Formulates policy	Sets example
Corrects weaknesses	Builds strengths
Does things right	Does the right things
Wields control	Applies influence

First, the skills and focus of a manager make a very important contribution to any successful organization. Depending on the situation, the traits and behaviors in both columns of table 3-1 can be extraordinarily valuable. To aspire to world-class results, an organization must have people who consistently master both foundational managerial traits and also leader traits. One metaphor is that these differing manager and leader traits are like tools in a toolbox. The most effective professional will select a tool based on the requirements of the immediate job, use it masterfully, and then place that tool back in the toolbox and select the next tool specifically for the next unique job. The key is to utilize what is most appropriate for the operational need. In today's competitive business environment, optimizing results requires not just managerial skills but also leadership skills.

Second, though managerial skills are critical, it is leadership traits that actually build employee excellence. The Chain Reaction of Excellence Model (see figure 1-1) shows how leadership excellence is the driver of employee engagement. The leadership quality of the influential people throughout an organization makes the difference in reaching its potential. Although achieving world-class results requires both, great leadership is an *extension* of effective management—and the reason the focus of this chapter is leadership, not management.

Lead through Influence

If you were asked to summarize all the key leadership attributes listed just above, you could distill them down to one word: influence. Influence is a power that creates enormous potential when combined with other leadership tools—much like water, which alone may not have much of an impact but when combined with eons of time can create something as profound as the Grand Canyon. Influence is one of the most effective yet least leveraged tools in your leader's toolkit.

It is easy to mistakenly consider someone a great leader who is in the top position of an organization. Far too often, society tends to have the most respect for those who are in positions of formal authority. Because of this, many people focus on simply obtaining the title of leader. They want to control the decisions that are made in their environment.

However, we would all do well to abandon this flawed perspective. Is it really about being in charge? Do control and force truly engage others in the workplace and create highly satisfied customers? Consider the pain of a parent who seeks to control everything his or her young child does, only to later face the consequences with a rebellious teenager who resists any attempt at control. Great parenting has little to do with power per se. Why is it different with organizations?

Let's consider an example. Think of a former U.S. president you would call great.

Whom did you name? Did someone like Zachary Taylor first come to mind? No? How about Franklin Pierce or Millard Fillmore? Or perhaps someone from a more recent century, like William McKinley or Calvin Coolidge?

Perhaps, like most, you named someone like Washington, Jefferson, Lincoln, or one of the Roosevelts? Perhaps someone more recent, like Kennedy or Reagan? Why do we typically think of these types of individuals more often than the Fillmore or Taylor types?

Here's the interesting thing: According to constitutional law, all U.S. presidents have had essentially the same span of power. So why does one president stand out above the others? By law, we know it isn't because they were simply in charge; otherwise, every president would be great. Great presidents have left great legacies because they were men of *influence*.

This reality of how influence is different from power becomes even more intriguing when you consider great leaders who had little or no formal power but enormous influence. What about people like Mahatma Gandhi or Mother Teresa? Clearly, they were leaders, but not because they were in control of an organization.

The truth is that real leadership has more to do with creating a greater span of influence than anything else. And how do you increase this leverage? You do it by embodying the qualities noted above, like listening and inspiring others.

This is particularly important for those who are positioned toward the bottom of the organizational chart. Great organizations reinforce the reality that every person on this chart must realize that he or she has a span of influence. Regardless of an employee's role, the more he or she exerts this influence, the greater the likelihood that all around that employee will be engaged in creating results that matter.

That's right: Every individual should be a personal leader of influence. This is the significantly different perspective on leadership of legendary organizations.

This new perspective or "lens" for seeing true leadership can be likened to a lighthouse. The original source of the light, the bulb, has a limited capability. But surround this bulb with reflective mirrors and it becomes far brighter and all very useful. Likewise, individuals in your organization should focus on how they can magnify their light for the greatest good.

One contemporary symbol of this magnifying influence is Robben Island. Are you familiar with Robben Island? It's off the coast of Cape Town, and for 18 years it served as the prison home for Nelson Mandela during his 27-year ordeal of imprisonment under apartheid. He worked side by side with other prisoners performing hard labor in a lime quarry. His prison cell was so small that a 6-foot-tall person would have to lie diagonally to fit inside. For those many years, that was his circle of control—but his circle of influence was, and is, much larger. He inspired the end of apartheid. He changed the continent of Africa forever. He influenced the world for good. Whether it's transforming a country or transforming a work team, developing real influence invariably leaves a legacy.

Simply put, it's not about what you control, it's about what you influence. Why does this matter? It is crucial, because if you want to become an excellent leader, you must stop thinking so much about what you can or can't control and focus on what you must do to create greater influence. Leadership excellence is about influencing others by doing the same things that we described in the list given at the beginning of this chapter of those qualities that are strongest in an individual who is a great leader—communicating a compelling vision, and all the rest.

Types of Leaders

Another aspect of effective leadership is implementing the right kind of leadership in the right circumstances. In general, there are three kinds of leaders: personal, spontaneous, and positional. Let's look at each, as diagrammed in figure 3-1:

✦ Personal leaders accept responsibility and act consistently to do their work as best they can each and every day. This may be the individual two cubicles over from you. That person isn't the manager, but he or she is always there when someone has to stay late, or when someone remembers your birthday, or simply when someone needs to get the job done well each and every time.

✦ Spontaneous leaders take initiative and see opportunities to lead in times of greatest need. Perhaps there is no greater example than the many men and woman who lost their lives helping others that fateful September 11, 2001. Though many were running out of World Trade Center, several ran back in, uncertain of the conclusion but knowing that people needed help. These are the ones who emerge in their greatness during moments of crisis.

✦ Positional leaders are the kinds of people many typically think of as leaders. They are simply those who lead from a position of authority. They have an opportunity to lead by virtue of their title. But a title alone does not a leader make. After all, can you think of someone who was not necessarily a manager but who acted as a leader in some personal or spontaneous manner? Vice versa, can you identify someone who is a manager but is far from exhibiting those characteristics described above as typical of a leader?

Figure 3-1. Types of Leaders

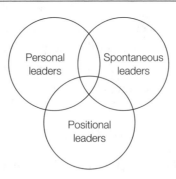

The bottom line is that organizations need more leaders, not more managers. Every employee can, and should be expected to, exercise some type of leadership. And when we say leadership, we again mean exhibiting those traits described above that influence others to do their very best. Lee Cockerell, the former executive vice president of operations for Walt Disney World, often said that "a person who has authority and doesn't use it is irresponsible." We are all obligated to use whatever influence we have to make a difference for the better. World-class leaders are constantly looking for ways to guide circumstances forward—they are continuously improving operations to achieve better results.

Next steps for understanding how to achieve leadership excellence:

✦ Start with a self-assessment. Gather accurate feedback about your skills and knowledge regarding influence, engagement, business fundamentals, and the like. Are you a role model in all that you do? Do you have integrity?

✦ Do you have an organizational goal about which you are passionate? Are you able to articulate your vision for reaching this goal in a compelling way?

✦ How engaged are you with your team? How engaged are the team's members with each other?

✦ Are you actively involved in developing new leaders within your organization?

Chapter 4

Using the World Class Excellence Model to Transform Your Business

To enable you to more completely understand and satisfy your customers, we have developed the World Class Excellence Model—shown in figure 4-1—to demonstrate the relationships between the various crucial components that bridge the corporate culture and the organizational brand. This model, which uses the traditional image of the sailor's compass rose and completes the image of the Customer Compass introduced in chapter 2, offers unique insights for helping leaders attain excellence within their organizations, particularly in building compelling customer brands and creating high-performing employee cultures. By showing how to unify your efforts for maximum efficiency and effectiveness, this groundbreaking tool will help you understand established, big-picture business strategy as well as proven best practice tactics. Let's look at each component of the model as shown in the figure.

Understanding Your Customers

The entire World Class Excellence Model is fully embedded in the customer experience. Typical businesses focus on knowing about their customers, but world-class businesses go beyond that—to understanding them, through the use of psychographic information, as discussed in

Figure 4-1. The World Class Excellence Model

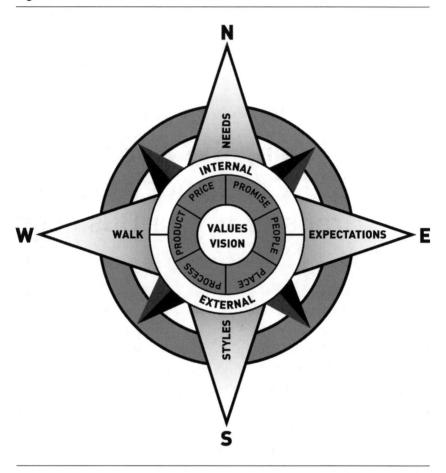

chapter 2 and shown in the Customer Compass aspect of the model. Another important distinction is that these businesses define their customers as including not only those whom they serve externally but also those who work for them internally. We cannot emphasize this enough: Your organization will change for the better when you broaden your concept of "customer" to include your own employees. Everything that successful organizations accomplish is aligned with the foundational aspects of the customers whom leaders serve (for descriptions of these aspects, see chapters 1 and 2).

As figure 4-1 shows—and as was explained in chapter 2—we represent this effort to understand people through using the analogy of a compass. To briefly recapitulate, just as you need a compass to direct you on a given path or journey, no organization can succeed without reading its Customer Compass. And likewise, just as the value of a compass rests on its directional points of north, south, east, and west, so does your Customer Compass—whose four points are needs, expectations, styles, and walk. In the following sections, we consider this model in detail. To best navigate the process, we begin at the center of the model shown in figure 4-1 and move outward, building on each concept and, in turn, providing strategic and tactical alignment (and integrity) for the entire organization.

Understanding Your Core Values and Vision

There is consensus among the most renowned organizations in the world. They all agree that understanding your core values and vision is the first and by far the most important step of any organizational improvement initiative. Its importance cannot be overestimated. It affects every aspect of the operation. It is indeed *the core*.

Tragically, all organizations that fail to adequately consider this vital component struggle without relief—and until they deal with the core, they are destined to continue to struggle. Understanding the core is not simply a mental exercise. World-class organizations use it as the foundational key driver for their strategic growth and their tactical day-to-day operations.

It is absolutely critical to invest significant time and effort in discerning the two components of the core: values and vision. Once established, they can be used as tools that will guide goal setting, decision making, identifying appropriate behaviors, setting the criteria for effective hiring, developing guidelines for training and development, justifying buy-in and engagement, identifying guidelines for rewards and recognition, and on and on. The innermost circle of the World Class Excellence Model shown in figure 4-1 includes your values and your vision. Let's look briefly at each, to explore what they are, how they are utilized as tools, and how to develop your own.

Values

Values are at the center of the model. They are a declaration of what you believe—whether personally or as an organization. Values are what we care most deeply about; they are the foundation of your corporate culture—ultimately driving behaviors and results for your company. Consider them the "why" of your organization. As David Cohen (2006, 7) states in his best-selling book *Inside the Box,* "What an organization stands for on the inside is equally as important as the vision it tries to make real to the world outside."

Most professionals make the mistake of taking values for granted—treating them as only a theoretical reality that they are obligated to identify for traditional internal corporate documentation. Those who adopt this naive position will establish a gap that will actually keep them from achieving any kind of significant success.

In their book on corporate culture and performance, John Kotter and James Heskett (1992) report cumulative research on 200 companies—as wide-ranging as Hewlett-Packard, Xerox, Nissan, and First Chicago—which showed that those companies that consistently valued and cared for their employees, customers, and stockholders had much faster growth in revenues and jobs than other firms over an 11-year period. The message here is that values are not simply nice to have. Organizations that shape their culture around their values will find themselves directly focused on attaining results.

There are two basic, distinct types of values: philosophical and operational. Philosophical values are the lists of conceptual words that many organizations put together today. Typically, these lists include words like integrity, honesty, respect, service, excellence, safety, quality, and teamwork. These are all very good concepts, but, for the most part, they lack usefulness. Generally speaking, philosophical values are concepts that (1) no one in the general population disagrees with (so why list them?) and that (2) are disturbingly the same for most organizations—regardless of industry. Simply put, though it doesn't harm a company to identify philosophical values, the real benefit is realized from operationalizing these values.

Operational values are tactical standards of excellence that articulate the goals for service behaviors throughout the organization. Thus operational values, as opposed to regulatory standards, are guidelines for the operation's service behaviors. The important thing that a world-class organization does differently from average companies is that it actively uses operational values as tools to create consistency among all its functions.

For instance, Michael F. DeSantiago, of Chicago's Primera Engineers, shares a story of how his firm was attempting to gain a foothold in the very competitive Chicago engineering talent pool against other firms that were bigger and more established: "One day, as we were preparing to interview a young engineer, I recall thinking how important it was to convey to this young professional our company values, not only the 'basics' such as salary, benefits, and the like. It seems clear to me that our consistent reinforcement of our 'QTIB' values has helped establish a culture in which adherence to *quality* is uncompromised, *teamwork* is exhibited every day, acting with *integrity* is nonnegotiable, and work/life *balance* is expected and respected" (DeSantiago 2009). For this engineering firm, it is notable that these values, which could have simply been philosophical, have been actively integrated into day-to-day operations.

Like philosophical values, operational values provide a target with which everyone in the organization aligns. Consistency is a key component in creating both a strong internal corporate culture and a clear, established external brand. An organization's operational values describe the nature of its desired day-to-day behaviors, so all employees have parameters for what behaviors are appropriate. Table 4-1 gives examples of operational values established by a number of different organizations.

A problem with operational values is that 99 percent of the companies that do develop them commit a serious blunder by failing to utilize them as a decision-making tool. For everyone in an organization to act consistently without adhering to some kind of "Stepford Policy," employees must have a tool that guides them when they are faced with a problem. If the operational values are all equally important, then it is highly unlikely that everyone in the organization will agree about what he or she should first respond to and why. World-class companies have discovered

Table 4-1. Examples of Operational Values Established by Different Organizations

Organization and Values	Thoughts and Considerations
Walt Disney: • safety • show • courtesy • efficiency	Conceived at a time when the stereotype was compared to carnivals and fairs, Walt Disney transformed the experience by introducing these values and aligning all behaviors in the operation to reflect them. More than 50 years later, this decision continues to create magic.
JetBlue • safety • caring • integrity • fun • passion	These values were created from the inception of JetBlue. They are introduced in its orientation—in fact, they are the first words employees see on the wall when they enter for orientation at JetBlue University in Orlando. These values have great application whether you are talking about the internal or external customer service experience. This makes alignment easier to attain.
Con-Way: • safety • integrity • commitment • excellence	It's hardly imaginable that a large trucking company like Con-Way would really bother with promoting values. But they have gone to great lengths to establish a culture that fosters excellence. As such, they have rolled this out as their constitution to more than 20,000 employees. Then they have established management tools, local task forces, celebrations, and reward/recognition programs.
Primera Engineers: • quality • teamwork • integrity • balance	For almost 20 years, Primera has actively used their values as a selection tool to recruit top talent. In addition, they have awards and periodic president-employee discussions specifically about the values and reinforcing their implementation.
Brookfield Zoo: • safety • courtesy • appearance • knowledge • efficiency	We invited the core team of this impressive institution to Walt Disney World to benchmark. The result was not only their service vision statement but also their service standards values (i.e., operational), which are listed here. You can see that they parallel Disney's, only that they changed "show" to "appearance" and added "knowledge" to emphasize the educational aspect of their organization.

that involving employees in prioritizing their operational values creates a predetermined checklist that results in a consistency of behaviors across all operational functions—reinforcing a branded customer experience.

Operational values are more than mere words—they are concepts that reflect an emotional connection to that which "has value." Think of values as "fuel" for action. When people don't care about the reason for a required behavior, they aren't motivated, and therefore it is typically very difficult to gain buy-in, ownership, and commitment. In this way, it becomes evident how using values as a tool can positively affect an organization's day-to-day operations. There are several important criteria for developing your own values:

✦ People who care deeply about your "reason for being" care about these values.

✦ These values spark an emotional reaction from your employees.

✦ These values accurately reflect the behaviors that you expect throughout your organization.

✦ These values are limited to an easily manageable number— typically between three and seven.

Establishing the purpose and motivation for your company's actions will generate the fuel for action, but a clear direction is required to ensure progress. This is where the second element of the core comes into play— the vision.

Vision

The vision is the "where" of the organization. Essentially, a vision is where you want be as a company. As a tool, your organization's vision should be a compelling goal just out of reach of your current capabilities. The hope is that the vision is articulated in such a way that people are inspired because it is founded on what they passionately value, and it describes (not too concretely) a place where they desperately want to arrive and that, if everyone works together effectively, can be reached someday.

People sometimes mistakenly consider a vision to be interchangeable with a mission statement. However, a mission statement centers on the present and is strictly operational. It's the "to do" aspect of how you articulate your culture. It focuses on your organization's fundamental purpose, identifying your customers and the critical processes for serving them. It may inform you of the desired level of performance.

A significant issue that becomes a real roadblock for most companies is the confusion between "vision" and "vision statement." Hundreds, perhaps thousands, of business books over the years have explored the nature of corporate visions. Unfortunately, people typically read portions of a book, assemble a task force, and come up with some words they like. Then they print up this statement in a nice typeface, frame it, hang it on the wall, call it a vision, and think they have accomplished "the vision thing." But they have been deceived, and their organization's operations will therefore suffer.

Those who guide organizations need to recognize that a vision statement is just a collection of words, framed on a wall or on a laminated card. There's nothing wrong with this—as long as it is clear that it is only a statement. Conversely, a real vision lives in the hearts and minds of your employees—it is what the people in your organization "want to be." This real vision is a catalyst for behavior. A framed plaque collecting dust very rarely inspires action. Instead of this static image, a real vision should

◆ Declare your organization's higher purpose.
◆ Create an external image of the organization.
◆ Communicate a message and priority internally.
◆ Be aligned with your operational values and Customer Compass.

A number of world-class organizations have mastered the art of creating compelling visions for their customers—visions that are operationally useful and from which we can learn; for examples, see the case studies that follow. Also, table 4-2 gives a few of the many other great organizational visions that are operationally effective.

The Walt Disney Company: "We Create Happiness"

One of the best examples of an operationally useful vision is from the Walt Disney Company. Once hired, each "cast member" (as Disney calls its employees) learns that, no matter what task he or she was hired to perform, every employee has the exact same *real* job: to create happiness, in keeping with Disney's motto, which expresses its essential operational value: "We create happiness."

A story told in the book *The Wonderful World of Customer Service at Disney* (Kober 2009, 16) makes this point well. Consider an 18-year-old popcorn seller. His task is to pop the popcorn, box the popcorn, and sell the popcorn. Pop, box, sell. All day long, the same task, everyday. Then, in a moment when he has no customers, he notices

Table 4-2. Examples of Various Organizations' Great Visions

Organization and Vision	Considerations
Ritz-Carlton: Ladies and gentlemen serving ladies and gentlemen	Conceived by Horst Schulze, Ritz-Carlton's former president, this is probably the best known of any visions, though Ritz-Carlton itself refers to it as a motto. It is a powerful, concise statement that lifts the esteem of employees, many of whom are international immigrants who come from meager circumstances. For Ritz-Carlton, the challenge is keeping this statement timeless, when in many contemporary locations, "lady" and "gentlemen" can seem like antiquated terms.
Darden's Seasons 52: Celebrating living well through seasonally inspired healthier dining	Seasons 52 focuses on an aging baby boomer market that wants to eat healthier without sacrificing great taste. There are four seasons and 52 weeks in a year, which emphasizes an ever-changing seasonal menu.
City of Sammamish: Building community together	Short, succinct. and tied to the business of running the city. Even more exciting is the fact that the entire city was involved in developing both this vision and operational values.
Woodland Park Zoo: We inspire, naturally	Again, short and concise. Woodland Park Zoo wanted to be more than about the animals—it wanted to create passion for the entire conservation cause.

two older women taking photos of each other in front of the castle. At this moment, he has two options. He can either continue focusing on his task and wait for customers to request popcorn, or he can exceed expectations and "create happiness" by offering to take a photo of the two women together. Imagine that they say yes, he takes their picture, they thank him, and he goes back to popping corn.

He's provided great customer service, but has he created happiness?

This true story continues. Three months later, one of the two ladies wrote a letter to the park's management describing how, a few months earlier, she and her sister had gone to Disneyland together, and while there, a popcorn seller had stopped working to take a photo of both of them in front of the castle. She goes on to mention that she and her sister had not been on speaking terms for 20 years. They had decided to come to the theme park and spend time reestablishing their relationship. The photo the popcorn seller took is now the only one of them together in 20 years. She wanted to express how his gesture had ended up being so very important to her and her sister's memories of each other.

Did the popcorn seller "create happiness"? Yes! And why? Because he was taught to do more than his task. He was taught to fulfill the deeper mission of the organization—in this case, "creating happiness."

What if, afterward, the popcorn seller was confronted by his manager about stepping away from the popcorn cart to take the photo—even when there was no line at the cart—because it "wasn't his job"? What do you think the popcorn seller is going to do next time there's an opportunity to create happiness? When faced with conflicting messages, most employees conclude that it's safer to do average (by-the-book) work, until a better job comes along. But world-class companies avoid this problem by engaging their employees to deliver a superior customer experience.

"We create happiness," a concept originated by Dick Nunis and Van France when Disneyland was first created, has endured until today. By shaping a vision in your own organization, you can build a practical ideal, a statement, that epitomizes your products and services. In their landmark book *In Search of Excellence,* Tom Peters and Robert Waterman (1984, 168) wrote:

> Whether or not they are as fanatic in their service obsession as Frito, IBM, or Disney, the excellent companies all seem to have very powerful service themes that pervade the institutions. In fact, one of our most significant conclusions is that, whether their basic business is metal-bending, high technology, or hamburgers, they have all defined themselves as service businesses.

The Office of Federal Student Aid: "We Help Put America through School"

Imagine the possibilities, even the power, when everyone is pointed in the same direction with the same higher purpose in mind. If there is a successful example of this, it might be found in, of all places, the federal government. The Office of Federal Student Aid (FSA) is responsible for billions of dollars in grant and loan money. If you've taken out a college loan for yourself or for your child, you have undoubtedly been affected by the FSA. When one of the authors was part of the Public Strategies Group, he labored to assist this bureaucratic entity so steeped in poor service that Congress created a mandate to enable it to become more customer focused. This mandate required the FSA to look at itself more carefully. It had been focused on compliance—making schools and financial institutions follow the rules—but focusing on the individuals who actually received the grant or loan was another matter.

Under the direction of a new leader, the FSA devised a new service theme: "We help put America through school." Here's an example of what this looked like operationally. An FSA manager was on summer vacation reading the newspaper when she noticed a letter to the editor from a mother who had been swindled by a private company that had promised to get her daughter into the college of her dreams. The letter described how, after spending two years and thousands of dollars, the daughter had not been accepted by any colleges due to the company missing several deadlines.

Upon learning of this mother's and daughter's experience, the FSA manager became enraged and immediately started making calls to those she knew in the college community. After several weeks, the daughter was not only enrolled in the prestigious university she dreamed of attending but had also been awarded some available scholarship funds. Although it was not the FSA manager's responsibility to handle individual student challenges, by helping this student, she was truly able to "help put America through school."

Guidelines for Developing and Implementing Your Core Vision and Values

How do you develop your core vision and values? There are seven key steps:

1. *Engage all your employees.* One of the best ways to get people focused on your core is to involve them in brainstorming, developing, and implementing the core message. Even if it takes several months, it's worth taking the time to involve everyone in establishing the core. Avoid trying to create it in a vacuum.

2. *Though philosophical values are important for both internal and external customers, operational values are especially pertinent to how you serve your external customers.* For instance, "teamwork" is a great organizational value for your employees, but it has little application to external customers. Though your customers may never see a list of operational values, they should be able to clearly identify your values by the great service they receive.

3. *Make sure that each value is unique.* Each word should stand alone as a distinct service term. For instance, "empathy" and "concern" could be considered too similar. Likewise, "confidence" and "privacy" are parallel terms. And even "respect" and "dignity" may be too close to each other to be meaningful as separate concepts.

4. *Create a prioritized order of values.* One practice the most successful companies share is that they have prioritized their operational values. This provides a tremendously valuable tool for facilitating decision making among your employees. The problem with most organizations is that if their values are all considered equally important, different opinions about priorities typically arise when employees try to solve a problem. But if there is an established, commonly understood priority of values, then all employees can follow a consistent problem-solving path. For example, if an incident occurs and the most important value of the company is identified as "safety," then everyone's first step is to gauge whether or not the situation is safe. If it isn't, they'll agree to take action to fix the safety consideration first. If the situation is already safe, they are guided to collectively consider the next-most-important value to solving the problem—continuing down the prioritized list.

5. *Ensure that your values encompass the organization.* The core should have meaning and relevance to everyone in the organization. To create integrity throughout the operation, there must be consistent values in every facet of the company. Some try to individualize these from area to area, but it's nearly impossible for the "back of the house" to support the "front of the house" effectively if each is focusing on different criteria. For instance, if the front-of-the-house team's primary workplace value is "speed" and the back-of-the-house team's primary workplace value is "accuracy," there are likely to be misunderstandings and strained interactions because what one team values is at odds with what the other team values.

6. *Make your values actionable.* Each value should encourage action. Values should not be grounded in esoteric theory; they should be tools for tactical application—focused on the customer or the employee. For instance, the value "courtesy" can easily be described

in behavioral terms and measured. "Grace," however, may be more difficult to articulate on a behavioral checklist.

7. *Keep your list of values brief.* Don't create too many, resulting in a long laundry list. To create values that can be a useful tool in day-to-day operations, benchmark companies limit the number of values to four or five—keeping them manageable and memorable for everyone in the organization.

It isn't enough to develop your core vision and values. You must also implement them. They must become part of your culture. Here are six key ways in which to do this:

1. *Announce them.* One of the best ways to get people to commit to your core vision and values is to involve them in developing and delivering the vision and values. Let your frontline employees deliver the messages, rather than the human resources department; or let them partner with capable facilitators. In many instances, they will be more credible than somebody from headquarters. Also, they will be the first to implement and support your core vision and values in their own working lives.

2. *Hire in keeping with them.* Use your vision and values as criteria for hiring employees with the "right fit." As new employees come on board, share with them the nonnegotiable nature of the core of your organization. It should be the most important element of any new employee's orientation.

3. *Promote them.* Post your vision and values everywhere—banners, posters, murals, wallet cards, newsletters, and so forth. Keep them in front of every employee. Don't let them simply be a plaque in a boardroom. Make them part of the fabric of your organization's daily give and take.

4. *Discuss them.* Successful, world-class organizations host regular team meetings. And at these meetings, rather than just speaking about the logistics of the day, they discuss how they can further their vision and values. They talk about how the situation looks in their own area, how it is lacking, and what they can do to improve it.

5. *Connect behavior to them.* Empower employees to work within the framework of your core vision and values. Teach them the principles that go with your core, and then let them govern themselves—with accountability. This will increase their engagement. Reinforce and support employees by recognizing and rewarding the behaviors that align with your core.

6. *Deliver your products and services in accord with them.* That's what the rest of this book is about—we're going to explore how your core vision and values can be brought to life when delivering your products and services. Your core values and vision essentially becomes a guide for your company's behaviors. All decisions about what you provide and how you provide it to your customers should be aligned with your core.

You can't just deliver service. You must align it with your core vision and values. That integrity is what will make you stand out above your competition. Alignment and integrity are what ultimately gives you a high-performing culture and a valued brand. That's why it's important to strategically develop your core vision and values, before starting implementation.

The Six Ps

> *What distinguished these unusually successful companies from their competitors was a measurable advantage in customer and employee loyalty. Each time we found a performance record that was hard to square with the traditional economics taught in business schools, we also found a company with superior loyalty. Each time we found a company with outstanding loyalty, we also discovered a company that was delivering superior value to its customers and employees.*
>
> —Frederick F. Reichheld, *The Loyalty Effect*

Moving to the second concentric circle of the World Class Excellence Model shown in figure 4-1, you see the six basic systemic concepts that all world-class organizations use to deliver the values and vision of their brands. Together, these six concepts—promise, people, place, process, product, and price, which we call the Six Ps—provide the basis for developing guidance and primary operational methods not only for serving external customers but also for internal operations. The Six Ps are summarized in table 4-3.

The ultimate goal is to have the people, product, place, and process live up to the promise, and be well worth the price. This can be illustrated with the Six Ps Customer Formula:

Promise < People + Place + Process + Product > Price

Unless all six of the Ps are considered according to this formula, the experience will not exceed the expectations of the customer, there will be no loyalty, and there will be no sustainable competitive edge. World-class organizations consistently balance these fundamental components of the customer experience—and consistently reap the benefits.

The cumulative components of the Six Ps in the context of the rest of the whole model have a direct impact on the experience of both the employees and the customers. In parts II and III of this book, we explore in detail how they can help you excel at exceeding the expectations of both your internal and external customers.

Table 4-3. The Six Ps

P	Internal (Culture)	External (Brand)
Promise	The organizational culture	The brand promise
People	Those serving those on the front line	Those serving on the front line
Place	The "backstage" setting for your employees	The "onstage" setting for your services and offerings
Process	Employee guidelines, rules, and policies	The policies, procedures, and rules that govern the delivery of your products and services
Product	The employee offerings you provide	The goods you offer to customers
Price	Tangible and intangible costs to the employees	Tangible and intangible costs to the customer

The concepts by which all services are delivered are the middle four Ps—people, place, process, and product. As an initial overview, examples of the service delivery tools derived from these four Ps that have an impact on the external customer experience are given in table 4-4.

As we mentioned above, because your employees are, essentially, internal customers, you can see how the same experiences from their viewpoint are shown in table 4-5. Note the similarity of approach—the model unifies and aligns all aspects of your operation to a single point of reference. All these topics are detailed in the chapters to come.

The Unity of External and Internal Experiences

Great organizations don't focus on isolated "moments" of service. They focus on the entire customer experience of multiplied moments—and, as mentioned earlier, world-class businesses view the customer both externally and internally, as shown in the outermost concentric circle of the World Class Excellence Model. Every aspect of the customer's

Table 4-4. Examples of Service Delivery Tools That Affect the External Customer Experience

Experience	People	Place	Process	Product
Taking a flight	• Flight crew • Reservationist	Plane Terminal	Boarding Policy	Flight
Spending time in a hospital	• Admissions • Surgeon • Nurse • Technician	Hospital Clinic	• Admission process • Payment procedure	• Open magnetic resonance imaging • Surgical procedure
Going to the store	• Cashier • Produce assistant	The store facility	Return policy	• Food • Sliced deli meats
Buying a car	• Sales representative • Financing representative	Car lot	Car inspection process	Vehicle
Buying wholesale	Minimal, to cut costs	Warehouse	"On your own" processes	Discounted merchandise

Table 4-5. Examples of Service Delivery Tools That Affect the Internal Customer Experience

Experience	People	Place	Process	Product
Working for an airline	Other members of your flight crew	• Plane • Layover hotel	Schedule	Employee emergency fund
Working in a hospital	• Fellow staff • Hospital administration	• Hospital • Clinic	• Admission process • Payment procedure	Personal discounts on pharmaceutical goods
Working in a grocery store	• Fellow employees • Stockholders	The store break room	Return policy	Retirement plan
Selling cars	Sales representative	Car lot	Hiring process	Personal vehicle discounts

experience either adds to or takes away from his or her perceived value—and dictates the likelihood that the customer will become a loyal advocate for the company and its brands.

Ultimately, the qualities of all the components of the World Class Excellence Model influence the value of the operation itself. In their book *The Experience Economy*, Joseph Pine II and James H. Gilmore (1999) explore the concept of "you are what you charge for"—in other words, if you compete solely on the basis of price, you become commoditized and offer little or no true differentiation. They offer an example about coffee. When coffee was seen as a commodity, one could purchase enough beans to make a cup for a penny or two. That changed when coffee was transformed into a "good" that could be ground, for a few additional pennies. In time, coffee also became a "service," and thus coffee shops began making customers cups of coffee, which were also eventually sold at corner convenience stores for about a dollar. The most recent coffee transition came with the advent of Starbucks, which led in creating an experience so powerful that people were willing to pay more than five times the convenience store price for a cup.

Although markets have softened and the demand for an expensive cup of coffee has receded, one thing has become obvious: Today's loyal customer cares most about his or her overall experience—so being world class must focus on all facets of every customer's experience. The essential question for every responsible leader becomes "How do we create an experience that not only lives up to its promise but also sustainably positions us ahead of our competition and enables us to make a significant profit?"

The ultimate goal is to have the people, product, place, and process live up to the promise, and be well worth the price. To bring this concept to life, world-class companies intently focus on connecting proven tactics with each of the Ps.

Building Brand and Culture

Employees yearn to be associated with an organization of which they can be proud. Many are willing to make extra effort to help their company achieve its goals—if they share the goals and values of its organizational culture, as illustrated by this quotation from *Branded Customer Service: The New Competitive Advantage* (Barlow and Stewart 2004, 128):

> Many business leaders maintain that their most sustainable competitive advantage is corporate spirit, employee engagement, and a belief throughout the organization in what it is trying to achieve. We are living in an age when intangible values are identified as key indicators of success. It is also a period when the most productive workers tend to be those who are engaged with and connected to the soul of the organization. It is estimated that a recent and minor drop in employee engagement in Singapore, for example, costs that company between $4.9 billion and $6.7 billion annually.

The models that world-class companies use to build their internal cultures of excellence are—not coincidentally—the same models used to create a strong brand. The secret is staying focused on the core vision and values and the six Ps discussed here. Every world-class organization has discovered that these aspects are inextricably linked—its internal dynamics create its external experience, which creates its reputation, which, when linked to the images representing its business, creates its brand—all aligned with its unique core vision and values. With the World

Class Excellence Model, for the first time, a single conceptual, experiential framework reflects the real-life dynamics faced both inside and outside the organization.

The Customer Compass

Beyond the concentric circles, the four points of the Customer Compass, which we explored in detail in chapter 2, form the outermost part of the World Class Excellence Model. To briefly review, this Compass has four "directional" points, which can be studied both strategically and tactically to identify and respond to every internal and external customer's unique qualities:

✦ *Needs:* Beyond the most basic needs to sustain life itself, people have needs that are more relevant to them and are often hidden—but still drive their purchasing decisions.

✦ *Expectations:* These are not concerned with your assumptions about your customers but with the preconceived notions customers have of your company; until you understand these expectations, you cannot hope to exceed them.

✦ *Styles:* People respond to your products and services based on their individual styles that affect how they interpret and value the service experience.

✦ *Walk:* You must walk in the shoes of your customers—and thus realize that the experiences of others that can influence your business choices toward what matters personally to them ultimately result in a more profitable bottom line.

Applying the Model: The Rest of the Book

In the context of the World Class Excellence Model, the next two parts of the book detail the delivery tools that leaders can use to create an excellent experience for both external and internal customers (employees). Part II focuses on the six Ps as they relate to an organization's internal experience, its culture; and part III focuses on how they relate to its external experience, its brand.

Next steps for using the World Class Excellence Model to build and apply your core foundation:

✦ What values distinguish you from those of similar employers? What values can create passion for what you do?

✦ What is your vision for what you ultimately provide your customers? Does this vision create passion? Does it differentiate you from your competition?

✦ How do you go beyond knowing about your customers to truly understanding them?

✦ What do your customers think you are promising them? Are you consistently delivering what you're promising?

✦ How well are your people, workplace, processes, and product exceeding the expectations of your customers? Are there any inconsistencies in the experience you are delivering?

✦ What is the true cost of doing business with you? Do you provide a clear value for your customers' investment?

Part II

Leading the Culture

Chapter 5

Proclaiming the Promise of Your Culture

To best serve your employees—P1, in the context of the World Class Excellence Model (see figure 4-1)—you must first proclaim the promise of your culture. Just as you attract customers with your promise of better products and/or services, you do likewise with potential employees—whether you are aware of it or not. You keep employees, sustain them, and support their—and your—success, based on how you deliver on these promises.

Typically, before considering employment, a potential employee becomes familiar with an organization from a variety of experiences—including being a customer. When a new employee begins his or her first day with the organization, he or she is there as the result of a series of interactions with the company—classified ad, phone call, interview, collateral material, and the like—all of which have helped the person to form some perception of what working there should be like and how good a fit he or she should be for the job. Once on the job, there will be countless other interactions—orientation, fellow employees, customers, internal collateral, work processes, employee-only locations, and so forth—that will reinforce (or undermine) the new hire's perception (or promise) he or she feels the organization has made to him or her.

Whether it is appropriate or not, human nature seems to lead employees to take perceived commitments personally—as was mentioned earlier regarding the customer relationship to the brand. Every day, organizations communicate information about their culture—whether by design or by default—to employees. Employees make important daily decisions that affect their job, and ultimately their career, based on these company "promises."

Like external customers, internal customers (employees) expect promises to be fulfilled. Employees have another expectation: to align themselves with an organization that actively supports values and ethics of which they can be proud. The only way to have a healthy, long-lasting working relationship with your employees is by fully supporting your promise. This effort involves four initiatives:

+ *Implementing beliefs and philosophies:* Ensuring that the values at the core of the organization are obviously supported and actually implemented in its day-to-day operations.
+ *Cultivating an attitude of excellence:* The state of mind aligned with the unique personality of the company, with a commitment to the higher standards necessary to achieve world-class excellence.
+ *Speaking the language:* Sharing a purposeful "best-in-class" language, represented through words and symbols, is a powerful manifestation of the intended culture.
+ *Keeping customs and traditions:* Every group has customary practices that keep its cultural history alive—meaningfully connecting it with its promise.

Let's consider a story that illustrates these aspects of supporting your promise. One interesting cultural norm at the Walt Disney Company is that leaders must stay connected with the real-time operation (as discussed in chapter 2, in relation to the importance of "walking in the shoes" of customers in the Compass Model). Walt knew that his managers needed to be out in the theme park, not behind their desks, so he purposefully modeled that responsibility every day.

Walt had an apartment built above the firehouse at Disneyland so he could have a place to stay as needed during his frequent park visits. In the evenings, he would walk the park during the third shift, pouring coffee for the workers at midnight. During the day, he was out in the park, interacting with cast members (employees) and guests (customers) alike, experiencing things firsthand.

One day, a Jungle Boat pilot failed to notice that he had a famous passenger. When Walt stepped off the boat, he walked up to the Frontierland supervisor, Dick Nunis, and asked, "What's the trip time on this ride?" Dick replied that it was seven minutes. Walt responded: "I just got a four-and-a-half-minute trip. How would you like to go to a movie and have the theater remove a reel in the middle of the picture? Do you realize how much those hippos cost? I want people to see them, not be rushed through a ride by some guy who's bored with his job" (Thomas 1976, 290).

Dick responded by asking Walt if they could share the next ride to discuss details. Dick and Walt rode one of the boats through Adventureland, and Walt explained how to conduct the trip. For a full week, the Jungle Boat pilots were timed with stopwatches, until they perfected the ride experience. When Walt arrived for his regular visit to Disneyland on the weekend, he walked through Adventureland without stopping. He did the same the following weekend. After three weeks, he finally took another ride on the Jungle Boat. When the boat returned to the dock, Walt surprised everyone by entering the next boat for another ride. He went around four times on each of the boats, eliminating the possibility that the operators had "stacked the deck" by planting the best boat pilots up front. After he emerged from the fourth and final trip, Walt provided his only comment: a thumbs-up sign to Dick Nunis.

Since then, the thumbs-up gesture has been a sign of great service in the Disney parks.

This story has numerous lessons for building the promise of your culture, including these important notions:

1. Managing by walking around the workplace. This is was a hallmark of Walt Disney's philosophy even before Disneyland was built. He often spent time walking through the animation studios at all hours. Animators would arrange their in-process artwork in such a way to see if Walt had come by the night before. Walt anguished over spending money on offices, because he wanted management in

the park. Even today, Disney's leaders are expected to work in the theme parks performing frontline duties during peak seasons of the year.

2. Training and development is a priority. The story reflects the importance of training others as an investment in future excellence. To that end, the Disney University would eventually become one of America's first corporate universities.

3. Promote from within. Dick Nunis, the frontline supervisor, went on to become the chairman of Walt Disney attractions worldwide—so the above story isn't about some obscure employee. It's a tale about how cast members can contribute from anywhere in the organization and become part of its leadership.

4. Thumbs up. This remains a quiet, nonverbal gesture throughout the Disney organization, meaning "well done" or "great job creating an excellent guest experience"—that is still practiced among cast members today.

Implementing Beliefs and Philosophies

Organizations are in business because they believe in the importance of providing a particular product or service in a certain way. Employees join these organizations because they share these beliefs. A world-class organization simply takes concrete steps to ensure that these common causes are brought to life for the benefit of its employees and the organization. Let's look at a few brief examples of how beliefs and philosophies can be implemented in action.

Among Google's corporate philosophies, two are "You can be serious without a suit" and "You can make money without doing evil." As Google grew and became a publicly held company, in 2006 its founders established the position of chief culture officer, whose purpose is to develop and maintain a corporate culture that is nonhierarchically flat and collaborative (Mills 2007).

The idea of IBM's "open door policy" stems from Thomas Watson Sr., who instituted the program back in the 1920s, largely to deal directly with employee grievances. This well-tested concept is still being successfully implemented by other firms, with impressive results. Adobe Systems uses this policy to maintain a culture of openness. The CEO answers emails within 24 hours, and employee councils provide management with ongoing ideas for improvement. At Facebook, the CEO's office has no door; he sits among the employees at a desk like other software engineers writing code, rather than occupying the traditional executive's corner office.

Although corporate beliefs often have deep roots, sometimes new traditions carry these beliefs to the next level. In 1997, the Methodist Hospital System in Houston added a new internal program called No One Dies Alone, which enables employees to volunteer time to spend with terminal patients. At the shoe manufacturing giant Nike, you may need your hiking boots instead of your running shoes. Shared priorities between the company and the employees sometimes mean that staff members must leave the office in Portland at inconvenient times to search for lost hikers and skiers on Mount Hood. When asked to explain this commitment, the firm's chief talent scout executive, Michael Leming, responds: "What's more important, saving lives or selling shoes?" (*Fortune* 2009).

David Neeleman spent time as a young man among poverty-stricken people in Brazil. While there, he experienced firsthand why it was important that all people be treated equally—regardless of socioeconomic status. In founding JetBlue, he implemented these same values. He felt that there should be no first class, that everyone should have an equally good experience. And he modeled this belief whenever he flew by taking his seat in the last row of the plane, because it was the one row in which you couldn't lean back. Later, he actually had the final row removed completely so that everyone could lean back. Another of his standard practices whenever he was a passenger on a JetBlue flight was to help the flight attendants serve drinks and snacks.

Cultivating an Attitude of Excellence

Winston Churchill said that "attitude is a little thing that makes a big difference." No words could be truer when it comes to creating a corporate culture. Employees are often attracted to certain organizations because of the attitude employees convey to their customers. For instance, it's hard to work effectively at Harley-Davidson if you aren't in sync with its very independent-style culture. It has achieved excellent results by manufacturing and selling motorcycles while still embracing that edgy "biker" attitude.

Contrast that with the Ritz-Carlton hotels, where there is an illustrious and sophisticated culture. This legacy is rooted in Cesar Ritz himself, a celebrated hotelier who sought to define himself as the "king of hoteliers and hotelier to kings." His philosophy of service was refined by his luxury hotel experiences in Europe. In the early years of running his hotel, guests were regularly checked to see if they were in the *Social Register* or *Who's Who* lists to distinguish the hotel as a uniquely elegant brand. In fact, potential guests writing to the hotel requesting reservations were sometimes turned down if the quality of their stationery was not suitable.

Another very unique attitude, though still maintaining a standard of excellence, is embodied by the work style of Southwest Airlines. According to Southwest, what sets it apart from all other airlines is its people; yet if you took all their employees and transferred them to another airline, the passengers wouldn't have the same superior flying experience. The attitude of Southwest Airlines' employees is the key. Their creed, known as "Living the Southwest Way," consists of three values (Barrett 2008):

1. *A warrior spirit:* This is found in demonstrating courage and hard work and in doing one's best.
2. *A servant's heart:* This is found in following the Golden Rule and treating others with respect.
3. *A fun-LUVing attitude:*. This includes having fun and being passionate about what you do. It also celebrates Southwest's roots originating flights at Love Field in Dallas, whose airport code is LUV.

People who apply to work at Southwest Airlines know what kind of culture to expect, because they have experienced a Southwest flight. Often, a person's motivation for working for an organization is grounded in his or her response to its corporate culture.

Speaking the Language

What's in a name? According to world-class companies that understand the value of communication when building their culture, language is critically important. Whether it is words, phrases, or even symbols, the style of language used has a tremendous impact on the organization's culture.

At the Ritz-Carlton, the carefully chosen language includes the phrase "ladies and gentlemen serving ladies and gentlemen." This expression is the catalyst for gauging the delivery of exemplary guest experiences.

Root Learning, an organizational learning and development consulting firm, was ranked as one of the top small workplaces by the organization Winning Workplaces. It refers to its employees as "Rootizens" and their workplace as the "Root-topia." Each year, it hosts a "Rooty" celebration.

Like other airlines, JetBlue refers to all employees as "crew members," but the term isn't simply a standard industry label. JetBlue places a strong emphasis on belonging as a member of a team. Reflective of their playfully engaging culture, all aircraft have blue as part of their name—and even their training simulators have the word "blue" incorporated into their title. JetBlue's crew members participate in the creative process and, ultimately, in selecting the names.

W. L. Gore & Associates provides fibers, cabling, fabrics, and filtration and pharmaceutical casing products to a wide variety of industries, from aerospace to heath care to manufacturing. The firm was recently recognized by *Fortune* magazine as one of the 100 best organizations for which to work. Its philosophy, known as the "Gore Method," has always been to be a team-based organization that fosters personal initiative. Its supervisors are referred to as "sponsors" rather than "bosses." In light of this title, there are no traditional organizational charts and no bureaucratic chains of command. Even performance reviews are based on a peer-level rating system.

At the Walt Disney Company, the language is a reflection of the very business they are in—entertainment and hospitality. At Disney, everyone is part of a show, whether "onstage" or "backstage." Employees are referred to as "cast members," and are "hosts and hostesses" to "guests," not customers. All 130,000-plus people in the organization refer to each other on a first-name basis, largely because founder Walt Disney preferred it that way.

Keeping Customs and Traditions

Traditions are the rituals that keep the corporate culture and morale alive. They manifest themselves differently depending on the organization. At Google, employees have an ongoing tradition of creating outrageous announcements around April Fool's Day. And you don't have to wait for spring to find Easter eggs inside a number of their software services. Clever surprises pop up as you navigate around the various services on their website.

Speaking of holidays, Southwest Airlines hosts a number of interesting customs and traditions. Among the most notable are the infamous Halloween celebration and the chili cook-off day. Though management will admit that little work gets done during these experiences, the benefits of these special traditions are an invaluable part of the Southwest culture. To this end, Pixar's Brad Bird, creator of *The Incredibles*, noted that

> in my experience, *the thing that has the most significant impact on a movie's budget—but never shows up in a budget—is morale.* If you have low morale, for every $1 you spend, you get about 25 cents of value. If you have high morale, for every $1 you spend, you get about $3 of value. Companies should pay much more attention to morale. (quoted by Hawn 2008)

What's true for a movie is also true for just about any organization. Each organization needs to have positive traditions that reinforce the culture, bring people together, and keep morale as high as possible.

Of course, there is more to organizational improvement than delivering a tradition such as a company picnic. One organization told us they nearly had an employee rebellion over their company picnic—and not just because they didn't like fried chicken or potato sack races. It was because the picnic had come to represent decisions made only at the upper management level without the input of the employees.

Traditions and customs are not a quick fix that will offset poor performance management issues, but they are proven tools for building effective organizational cultures that get world-class results. For instance, UPS, like Disney and other organizations, still promotes a significant number of its frontline staff members up to the executive ranks. Typically, world-class companies promote about 70 percent of all leadership positions from within their frontline ranks. Other organizations, like Starbucks, require newly hired executives from outside the company to work for months in frontline café positions before beginning their leadership role. This action ensures that the new leader is fully aware of the culture of the organization and can relate to the issues that reside at frontline levels.

Summing Up

Every organization has a corporate culture, whether on purpose or by accident. The real question is whether what you promise your employees is what you consistently deliver—every day. Culture, by design, suggests that you look at your traditions, attitudes, language, and philosophies and make certain that they are what you really want to be.

It was Abe Lincoln who said "We must not promise what we ought not, lest we be called on to perform what we cannot." No words could be truer as we move forward into the next chapters. The people, place, process, and product must all deliver on the promise. World-class organizations ensure that what they deliver is equal to or greater than what they promise. Moreover, the price must not be greater than what we promise or deliver.

Next steps for building the culture through promise:

✦ What philosophies describe the culture you are promising your employees?

✦ Describe the espoused attitude of your organization. Can potential applicants see this attitude in what you say and do?

✦ What vocabulary, expressions, or ideas underscore your culture?

✦ What traditions celebrate your history and culture?

✦ What stories do you share that underscore what your culture is all about?

Chapter 6

Engaging Employees for Service Excellence

Service-focused behaviors—P2, people, in the context of the World Class Excellence Model (see figure 4-1)—will make or break the experience for the employee. As Elizabeth Norberg, senior vice president of human resources for Dolce Hotels and Resorts, explains, "the internal culture gives the identity to the experience and the brand. Our culture is defined by our talent who really are the 'faces, arms, and legs' of the brand" (Norberg 2009). Nurturing this human "resource" is a critical action for world-class organizations.

For instance, the Walt Disney Company has not only identified front-line service behaviors but has also focused on those behaviors expected of its leaders in dealing with "cast members" (employees). Extending beyond the foundational cast member behavioral responsibilities, these leadership behaviors, called the Disney Leader Basics, align with the Chain Reaction of Excellence (see chapter 1). Let's look at a few examples of these leadership behaviors:

✦ Demonstrate commitment to their cast members—"Actively listen to the cast, and follow up on their issues as quickly as possible."
✦ Master the operational aspects and teach them to cast members—"Collaborate with partners from all lines of business to ensure a seamless guest and cast experience."

✦ Lead improvement in cast and processes—"Examine practices, remove barriers, and identify improvements in the daily operation."

Note that the Disney Leader Basics guidelines are not called "Disney Manager Basics." This was not an accident. Disney recognized that to truly optimize its potential it must strategically set the bar beyond the management skills to include the people influencing skills of leadership (explored in part I of this book). The goal was to provide better guidance to align employees' and leaders' behaviors, while providing a foundation that guided employees toward personal leadership.

Consider the Disney Leader Basics and ask "What if these guidelines were followed by all the frontline cast members?" That is the Walt Disney Company's hope. Though there is certainly some management-like language included, an organization where every employee is practicing personal leadership behaviors creates a phenomenal culture—like that for which Disney is known.

In keeping with this approach to people for which Disney has become legendary, this chapter explores how to engage your employees and thus lead them to deliver service excellence. We'll be considering these service-focused behaviors:

✦ Serving your employees.
✦ Building your culture with selection.
✦ Onboarding effectively.
✦ Focusing orientation on brand and culture.
✦ Making training and development a priority.
✦ Leveraging service huddles.
✦ Transforming employees into leaders.
✦ Maximizing the impact of rewards and recognition.

Serving Your Employees

Just as opportunities exist to individualize the branded customer experience, the same exists within the culture as well. Whether it is birthdays, anniversaries, or simply helping people who are down on their luck, seeking out opportunities daily to give time to others pays off—for the organizational ledger and beyond.

Here's one simple example. Con-Way's service center managers go out of their way to provide food and beverages for its drivers on days when the temperatures are extreme. This gesture is well received by its truckers, who come from an industry that doesn't typically support employees in such a personal manner.

Building Your Culture with Selection

One of the most critical aspects of a successful business operation is hiring talent that has the "right fit" to build results and leadership within the organization. Once a company has established its values and vision, the way to bring these concepts to life is to ensure leaders and employees act on them.

George Miliotes—the director of beverages and service at Darden Restaurant's Seasons 52—shared his philosophy about hiring the right people. One simple tactic is to ask a couple of questions. He asks them what they like about the food and beverage business … and times them. After more interview questions, he'll ask candidates what they do not like about the food and beverage business … and time them again. He claims that comparing the amount of time they spend answering these two questions (assessing the content of the answers as well) has been a great litmus test for determining which applicants have the passion required to excel in his demanding restaurant environment.

In addition, here's the advertising copy from a recent Nordstrom ad (with some phrases italicized for emphasis):

> We are currently looking for individuals with a *positive and energetic* attitude who are interested in sales, stock, or customer service positions. Key responsibilities:
>
> - Sales people provide great service through positive interactions and product knowledge with *each and every customer.*
> - Customer service representatives *meet our customers' expectations* with professional, efficient service at the point of sale.
> - Stock people *support our customers* by keeping our fixtures full with merchandise that is accurately ticketed.

On the basis of Nordstrom's widely known brand, it can be expected to be looking for customer-savvy individuals who are positive and energetic. However, this isn't an ad for a typical full-size Nordstrom store. It's an ad for a Nordstrom Rack, which is essentially a clearance outlet store.

Most "off-brand" operations do not require the same criteria for employment as their core branded operations. It is common practice to send second-rate employees to work at these kinds of bargain shops, so it might be expected that Nordstrom would do the same. But it does not. It has learned that settling for less undermines that particular operation as well as the brand itself—especially when its reputation rests on the delivery of an extraordinary customer experience.

At Nordstrom, the culture and resulting brand emphasize customer service. Your company's niche may be creativity or some other core value. Essentially, the degree to which new hires are aligned with the elements of your culture is the degree to which there will be operational integrity within the organization.

At Walt Disney World, they've used an effective process whereby candidates help self-select who is the right fit for the culture—a focus few job seekers consider. When visiting the Casting (Employment) Center, prospective cast members were offered snacks and drinks and then shown a brief video that highlights the four nonnegotiable requirements for working at Walt Disney World—before they even fill out an application. These four criteria created an acronym that supports the term "cast member":

- ✦ C—compensation: The pay for frontline employees is set to a schedule. Disney doesn't pay high wages—just a little above average for each job (about the 55th percentile).
- ✦ A—appearance: Based on the customer experience Disney strives to produce, it demands very specific appearance guidelines that may require potential employees to look a certain way for their role.
- ✦ S—schedule: Disney's labor demands are reflected in its philosophy: "We work while others play." Not only is its operation busiest during holidays and weekends, but any new hire will have the least seniority of more than 60,000 cast members.

✦ T—transportation: Because Walt Disney World is located outside most public transportation networks, cast members must have their own reliable transportation to satisfy the ever-changing scheduling requirements of this huge entertainment complex.

Here's the world-class difference: Instead of hiding the potential "deal breaker" issues, as do most employers, Disney actually leads the process with this information. Managing expectations at this juncture serves a very important purpose in the relationship with the future employee. After the video ends, the doors of the theater open and participants make a decision to interview or not. A total of 10 to 15 percent of those watching the video will self-select out (saving company costs for processing labor and materials), leaving the rest who are probably a better fit for the unique Disney culture.

Finding talent with the right fit at places like 24-Hour Fitness doesn't require a video. The firm's research showed that up to 80 percent of its new hires were coming from its own club membership—people exercising regularly at its gyms. One way for it to make better hiring decisions strategically was to shift its recruitment resources to its club members on the floor to identify a potential associate rather than on focusing on standard hiring techniques. This solution attracted the people with a healthy lifestyle who were most interested in this kind of work environment for a career.

Effective Onboarding

"Onboarding" is a term used to describe the timeframe from the hiring of a new employee to the end of his or her probationary period. The common trend for organizations, according to decades of exhaustive research, is that the highest level of turnover occurs within the first 90 to 180 days after a newly hired person starts working. Interestingly, the top reasons given by employees for leaving so quickly—across all industries—are that "the culture wasn't what I expected" (or "was promised") and "I didn't feel like I belonged."

Designing a supportive transition for all new hires will provide them the sense of belonging and reinforces the culture all at the same time.

Not only will this focus help the new employee, but it will also involve the existing employees and encourage a relationship while reinforcing the components of the culture for them. Shelby Scarbrough, past board president of the international Entrepreneurs' Organization, comments: "When you teach the 'why' behind the 'what,' you get better results—as it helps your team make better decisions in the future when they encounter similar situations" (Scarbrough 2009).

At JetBlue, because many crew positions require extensive travel, family members are actually invited to join orientation sessions for new employees. JetBlue has found that this investment in educating family members enhances support for both the employee and the employee's family's passion for and commitment to the organization—even from home. One interesting side benefit is that a high percentage of family members are convinced to join JetBlue as crew members themselves. Acting innovatively and strategically has created a very nice human resources benefit for JetBlue.

When the St. Regis luxury hotel opened in San Francisco, the entire staff was required to attend an orientation session that introduced them both to the facts and figures of working at that hotel and also to a carefully orchestrated exploration of their brand and culture. Numerous employees mentioned that they had worked at other upscale hotels in that area but had never before experienced anything that helped them understand the why and how of achieving world-class excellence. The payoff of investing in establishing a solid foundation is clarity of purpose, confidence in execution, and a passionate, unified team.

World-class companies find that what make the difference are several best practices—many of which involve encouraging relationships between new hires and star players. Here are some examples of useful onboarding ideas:

+ Each new hire receives an onboarding notebook, complete with handy tips to getting settled during the transition, including who to call for different questions—even local restaurants.
+ Adopt-a-New-Hire program—create a mentoring partnership with a role model. (What better way to "imprint" desired behaviors in the new employee!)

✦ Arrange lunches with different related departments once a week for the first six weeks.

✦ Schedule one-to-one meetings with the leader at regular intervals—the first day, first week, first month, second month, third month.

✦ After 60 to 90 days, have the new hire "teach" the team about what worked well and what could be improved regarding the onboarding process.

Focusing Orientation on Brand and Culture

After the interviewing and selection experience, the new hire's orientation is the first substantive experience with the organization's culture. It is important to design an orientation experience that "brings your culture to life." This experience sets the context for the employee's entire relationship with the company. Approach this vital phase in the development of your new "investment"—as if this was the only "handbook" he or she will ever receive about the company's culture, values, and vision.

Any organization can create an effective orientation program by developing an experience that introduces the brand and culture in such a compelling way that employees will continually refer back to it. Hospitals, couriers, government agencies, and even zoos have strategically aligned their own orientation to the brand and culture. For instance, Starwood Hotels and Resorts has created an international brand/culture/leadership experience that introduces more than 125,000 employees at more than 1,200 properties worldwide in their Sheraton, St. Regis, Westin, and Four-Points Hotels by Sheraton operations. Though the Starwood orientation initiative spans all the company's facets, the emphasis is firmly on establishing its culture. "All our research and data consistently supported the same findings—that designing a culture requires consistently linking everything together," states Allison Barber (2009), Starwood's vice president of talent management. "Orientation is when our associates can start connecting the dots. If they understand our core values, our guest focus, and how to behave in an on-brand way, then our guests will be happy, our associates will be successful, and Starwood will be successful."

When developing your own orientation experience, consider the following:

✦ *Position at the beginning:* Seriously consider requiring all employees to go through orientation *before* they can report to their work location. Many businesses will simply schedule a new employee to go through orientation when a class-sized number of new hires have been collected. This throws "unoriented" people "into the fire," which means they start their work experience in a very confusing way. This damaging first impression is a key contributor to the high turnover rates within the first few months. Postponing the orientation session to a later date also sends the message that the orientation information is not really that important.

✦ *It's about the culture:* Don't repeat the common mistake that average organizations make by filling their orientation programs full of tedious compliance information. The focus must be on making an emotional connection with your new hires. Creating inspired and passionately motivated employees is the most important strategic investment. The additional safety/ethics/regulatory information is important, but that can be conveyed afterward.

✦ *Model the brand/culture:* When designing an orientation program (or any training program, for that matter), make sure the methods used mirror the company's brand/culture. If you want a corporate culture of informal fun, then make the class informally fun. If you have a more formal culture, then the training should be appropriately formal. This is a great opportunity to have star frontline workers deliver this introductory information. The best advertisement for your company is a successful colleague who is living the work they are hiring for, and who exhibits a great attitude about making a difference. This reinforcing/modeling of your culture creates alignment and integrity from the very beginning.

✦ *Gather input:* The best people to determine what information and experiences should go into the orientation program are recently hired employees, your human resources team, and star employees who do an excellent job of personifying the values and culture of your organization. The more relevant the experience, the better investment it will be in creating your culture by design.

✦ *Build on your heritage:* An excellent way to arrange the flow of your orientation is to first explore your company's big picture (the past: history, founder, values, culture, and the like), then continue with more detailed information (the present: current vision, mission, operations, and the like), and then growth plans and expectations for the future. This process provides a strong foundational understanding of where you've been, where you are, and where you are going—all communicated operationally so employees can orient themselves and be best prepared for the on-the-job training phase.

Many types of tactics can support the orientation and onboarding experience. For instance, hoteliers like Four Seasons and Ritz-Carlton know that some of their new staff members have never enjoyed the quality of customer experience they deliver, so as part of the onboarding process, they provide opportunities to experience the hotel from the guest's perspective. This can include staying at the hotel for free, having their vehicle parked by a valet, dining at their restaurants—anything that will help the new hire truly "walk in the guest's shoes."

Many employees of the United Services Automobile Association do not come from the military, yet its focus is entirely on providing insurance and financial services to people in the Armed Services and their families. As part of its orientation, its new "recruits" are deployed with backpacks and military helmets. In an effort to understand the voice of the customer as part of the orientation, they eat military rations and read real letters from the troops deployed to "hot zones" around the world. For many, the experience invariably becomes an emotional one.

Making Training and Development a Priority

The costs involved in properly training your workforce are significant. A story that has become common in human resources circles begins with this question: "What if I spend money on training an employee and he or she leaves?" The insightful response: "What if you don't train him or her, and they *stay?*" Unfortunately, the world is full of organizations that choose to limit training and then, curiously, remain confused as to why their results are subpar.

In difficult times, most businesses make the critical error of cutting the development of the very (human) resources that determine the status of the customer relationship and resulting loyalty. The natural consequence of viewing training as merely an expendable support function is critical vulnerability. World-class organizations acknowledge the development of their people as not just an obligation but also an investment in gaining a competitive edge for a successful long-term future.

Many world-class leaders claim that effective training is the key to generating sustainable bottom-line results. The increased effectiveness of the employee's skills, knowledge, and attitudes toward customers and job functions far outweigh the initial investment, especially when it comes to the increased morale and loyalty that the company gains by implementing a strong training and development strategy.

If we again consider the framework of the Chain Reaction of Excellence Model (see chapter 1), world-class organizations know that the quality of the leader dictates the quality of the employee, which dictates the quality of the customer experience and the business results. Creating a competitive edge by optimizing the talent the organization's human resources doesn't happen by accident. Growing your organization's capabilities is only possible by growing the abilities of your employees. It's that simple.

For example, at the Container Store, professional training for first-year, full-time employees consists of 241 hours, a stark contrast to the industry average of 8. To supplement this, each store has its own full-time trainer. According to their operations and finance executives, the return far surpasses the investment.

Essentially, it comes down to a matter of integrity. Though almost every company claims that "our people are our most important resource," the investment of time and training dollars at the vast majority of businesses doesn't validate this claim. Employees hear and see these kinds of claims, but they also observe the contrary meager investment, and this can undermine their faith in their employer—and undermine the company's effort to achieve world-class excellence.

One important truth to consider is that training and development do not have to be expensive—or even be conducted in a formal classroom setting—to be effective. World-class organizations find low-cost or no-cost ways to develop employees. Consider the following:

- *Lunch and learns:* Generate a list of important topics and skills in which the employees are interested and then identify employee(s) who are role models of excellence for each topic or skill. Invite the star employee to prepare a 10- to 20-minute presentation of insights with an opportunity for questions and answers. Not only will the team have a free opportunity to learn something it has determined to be important, but your model employee will also have an opportunity to experience a time of genuine appreciation from his or her colleagues. (Another version of this idea is to have everyone meet for lunch once every week or two and ask attendees to talk for 5 minutes on a topic they have encountered that week, via a book, magazine, TV, or the like. This is followed by a discussion period.)

- *Video series:* Use the same format as described above, but utilize a film from a range of established training videos out on the market. Videos can be borrowed from the library or other sources. Invite a manager to host the film and to facilitate a discussion afterward.

- *Free local seminars:* Arrange to have transportation take selected employees to a local development opportunity and have them report back (at a lunch and learn?) on the insights they gained to help those unable to attend.

- *Expert sharing:* Partner with other local businesses in a "quid pro quo" sharing of experts. Schedule a leader or expert from outside your company to come in and present information of value to your employees. Arrange to have a leader or expert from your company return the favor.

✦ *Book reviews:* Distribute book reviews to your team. Give them a week or so to read the book, and then meet to discuss how the information could make a positive impact on the operation.

Leveraging Service Huddles

One action taken by nearly all successful organizations is that they gather work groups together to "get on the same page"—often called a pre-shift meeting or a team/service "huddle."

The value that a service huddle brings is that, in a very short amount of time, everyone on the work team can be made aware of current circumstances (for example, special things happening that day), get focused on challenges facing them (setting goals for sales, behaviors, and so forth), and create an opportunity for two-way communication.

One consistent practice among the best of the best organizations is the use of some sort of "toolkit" that introduces company concepts and commitments (related to its values, vision, the six Ps, a current initiative, or the like), with the opportunity to practice behaviors and give and receive feedback.

Ritz-Carlton has distinguished itself by hosting its version of such service huddles, known internally as a daily lineup. Each day the entire organization—worldwide—holds a pre-shift meeting. In this setting, those attending address one of the organization's values that are critical to service. It doesn't matter if you are in culinary services or housekeeping, or whether your hotel is in Boston or Dubai; everyone discusses the same Ritz principle on that day. There is power in the fact that everyone in the worldwide organization is focused on the same issue day in, day out.

The more relevant and powerful benefits arise when companies actively cater to their employees needs. Starwood hotels like Sheraton, St. Regis, Westin, and Four Points by Sheraton have modeled this by providing their management with a toolkit that centers on a larger number of critical topics. Like a recipe box, managers can take from that toolkit those topics that best fit the needs of their employees—all dictated by the real-time needs of that particular team.

The president of the Container Store delivers a weekly message in which the preceding weekend's sales are discussed and that week's new initiatives are emphasized. Beyond that, each morning the employees discuss the day's objectives as well as the previous day's results, which are posted for all to see.

Nordstrom in Orlando has a morning "pep rally" meeting that borders on a game show format. With music blaring, there is much celebration and recognition attached to the previous day's sales. Games and prizes are awarded. Customers' letters are read, and milestones acknowledged. The interesting thing is that the employees, most of whom work on commission, voluntarily attend these sessions, even though they are not formally compensated for doing so. Not only is the information relevant to them on a daily basis, but the team building and camaraderie also makes for a great start to the day. To accommodate the second shift, the manager holds a smaller-scale version for the late afternoon team out on the loading dock in the back of the store. One wonders what every other store in the mall is doing to focus its employees on results before the doors open and the customers come in.

Transforming Employees into Leaders

It has often been said that a business's success or failure depends on leadership. World-class organizations support this philosophy 100 percent; however, they approach leadership a bit differently than do other businesses.

First, leaders approach leadership development as an investment, regardless of the position—just like any other mandatory commitment for growth and success. Second, they understand that the responsibility of all leaders in the organization is to develop other leaders. Not only does this approach develop leadership skills and abilities throughout the organization, but it also "fills the pipeline" with a wealth of viable options when considering succession planning.

Though leadership development is, on some level, the same as any development efforts, there are some differences particular to the leadership role. These differences usually appear under the category of strategic skills and span every aspect of an organization's activities.

Maximizing the Impact of Rewards and Recognition

Although intrinsic motivation is always the best reinforcement of positive behaviors, external forms of rewards and recognition are a way of showing that you care for employees who contribute to the realization of company goals.

When it comes to rewards and recognition, world-class companies have one thing in common: They clearly connect the reward with the behavior getting the results (and the results are defined by the values and vision/goals). Reinforcing behaviors and employee contributions will (1) show that the company is "walking the talk" with regard to what it values, (2) increase the likelihood that the rewarded employee will repeat the desired behavior(s), and (3) provide an incentive for other employees to model those same behaviors—all of which is beneficial in guiding the team toward the common goal.

One intriguing pattern shared by the world's most successful businesses is that their primary source of rewards and recognition is *not* monetary. Unfortunately, an opposite approach has taken hold in mainstream businesses—whereby money becomes the sole reward system, and the resulting employee focus tends to be the money (and, therefore, not the customer). Eventually, the reward is simply spent on forgettable items such as bills. Consistent monetary rewards (again, if money is used as the primary source of rewards) eventually come to be seen as an entitlement—the power of the reward itself is negated, meaning wasted money, wasted time, and an active undermining of the behaviors desired for success.

A far more effective way to approach rewards and recognition is to focus on delivering *symbols of value*—like certificates, service pins, and statues—that represent a value much higher than the cost of the actual item given. For example, a small gold-colored pin may cost $5 if bought in bulk and will be worth $5. But if this same pin is used to reward a peer-nominated Employee of the Year, suddenly its value (measured by the contribution and esteem given with the honor) becomes priceless. The key component is to purposefully connect the positive behavior (what is being rewarded) to the positive impact in helping to move the company toward its goals (why it is being rewarded).

One tool becoming more popular is to begin a team database of sorts, collecting employee performance and personal information about how they like to be rewarded. An executive with a leading corporation shares the story of how he "didn't have a clue where to start" to recognize his employees, so, based on a mentor's suggestion, he obtained a set of 3×5 index cards. On one side of each card, he wrote an employee's name and all the value that he or she was bringing to their team (special projects they were working on, a particular trait that had helped the day-to-day operations, and the like). The executive then talked with the corresponding employee—such as finding out about their hobbies and favorite foods—recording all the information on the card after the discussions. The final step was to identify a positive behavior worthy of recognizing and then link it to a way that person liked to be rewarded, and then actively start recognizing.

For example, if Employee A liked movies, then the executive would buy two movie tickets, mention that he noticed how the employee was working a lot of overtime to make sure the project was on target, and suggest that the employee take his wife to the movies as a special thank-you on behalf of him and the company. Other options could be plants, pizza, and the like—all depending on what low-cost or no-cost "treats" the employee likes. This approach personalizes the reward and transforms an inexpensive token into a significant symbol of meaning—sure to leave a motivating impression.

New York City's Department of Finance made recognition a focus in its leadership programs with managers. When participants would discuss this, they would initially start venting about how little control they had to provide raises and bonuses. However, when asked to brainstorm all the formal and informal ways to recognize others, they immediately came up with scores of creative ideas they could easily implement.

That said, talking about recognition and implementing it are two very different matters. The commissioner of the Department of Finance, Martha Stark, directed the building of a "Cheers for Peers" intranet website, where anyone within the organization could go online and recognize the work of a coworker connected to the agreed-upon behavioral criteria. Each recognized individual would be presented with a small memento and then put into a monthly drawing for a gift certificate. The message is: Empower everyone to recognize others for the real results they produce.

Any serious effort to build up the culture requires intense focus on the most important resource of any organization: its human resources. Far too often, companies spout marketing campaigns about how they value their employees that are, in reality, mere lip service. Talking about valuing employees without doing it can actually be worse than saying nothing at all about the issue.

As proven by every consistently successful organization, treating your internal customer (employee) with the same care and effort as your external customer pays tremendous dividends. Although relationships can be one of the most complex and difficult aspects of running a business, they are also one of the most critical to get right.

Next steps for building the culture through people:

+ What criteria do you use to hire people? How important is it that they have the human relations skills to do the job? Is it required that they reflect the organization's values and standards?
+ What appearance guidelines are in place to ensure that your organization makes the right professional impression?
+ How can you empower your employees to be accountable for the entire service experience and not just their specific area of operation?
+ What low-cost or no-cost ideas can you use to reward others? What can you do to make recognition genuine and personal?

Chapter 7

Optimizing Your Workplace for Team Results

When optimizing the workplace—P3, place, in the context of the World Class Excellence Model (see figure 4-1)—there are areas and activities that your external customers should never see:

+ areas unsafe or dangerous to them
+ areas that do not pertain to the customer experience
+ certain operational activities meant to be carried out away from their presence
+ discussions that should not be held in front of the customers
+ areas that permit employees time away from the customers to "let their hair down"
+ employees on a break.

Imagine the impact at Walt Disney World if you were a guest and approached Cinderella, only to have her turn toward you smoking a cigarette and drinking coffee on her break. The effect would be shocking! Obviously, employees (including entertainers who portray fantasy characters) need to take breaks—and legally, of course, have the right to do so. To consistently give great service, they must be suitably rested and mentally prepared. To accomplish this, they need to be able to get away at times from those they serve, whether internal or external customers, during their shift to a break area—which may be a virtual or physical place where the employee can vent, handle personal needs, or simply relax without being "on" for their customers. If there's no opportunity for employees to appropriately exhibit "offstage" behaviors, they will exhibit them anyway—on stage, where there will likely be a negative impact on your external customer experience.

We refer to this situation as separating the "front of the house" (facing external customers) from the "back of the house" (employee-only areas). In most organizations, the two groups are divided and rarely interact with each other—despite the fact that they both exist to mutually support the external customer experience. To begin the process of unifying these two groups, many world-class businesses have begun referring to the "back of the house" as the "heart of the house"—acknowledging that the external customer experience would be impossible without the internal support team successfully delivering the promised products and services. Frankly, we really like this distinction. Unifying these two groups into a single, high-performing team is the first step in creating a culture of world-class excellence. One vital aspect of this effort is to support the employees by clearly identifying what the external customer should and should not experience. This is also known as separating "onstage" from "backstage." The key is to control the configuration of the workplace so that the customers—both external and internal—only experience what adds value for them. As simple as this concept may seem, it is one that few do well—and businesses suffer because of it.

Have you ever noticed that at many retail operations, employees take breaks in the front of the building? What message does it send to have employees taking a break in full view if there are long lines with customers waiting? The bottom line: If employees don't have a place to vent, relax, or let their guard down, they will eventually do so—in front of customers, thus undermining the value of the customer experience.

Sometimes, there may be back-of-the-house areas that are open to customers. One example of this might be a general manager's office. When the operation requires this situation, there must be an additional element of public presence, in the sense that they are clean and contribute directly to (and don't distract from) engaging customers.

It's Not about the Furniture

With respect to the heart of the house, consider the typical office environment. To truly engage employees and create a culture of excellence, most ordinary companies assume that they should spend their resources on expensive furniture or extravagant office perks. This flawed thinking has nearly always created the opposite effect from what was intended.

When it comes to the workplace and the experience for employees, it's not about the size of the office or cubicle, or the coffee machines or foosball tables. These "things" on their own do not help employees perform better as a team or achieve higher levels of operational performance.

Make no mistake: It is critical to have the resources necessary to do the job well—whether that means serious hardware and software or the resources necessary to travel freely or to make the right impression. The goal must primarily be to create an environment that best keeps the focus on the customer, product, and service. Many leaders have made the painful mistake of trying to "buy" the engagement of their employees with furniture and other gadgets. But this is the proven reality: What works best is understanding the true needs of internal customers (the employees) and giving them the tools they need to exceed the expectations of external customers. Using the Customer Compass (see chapter 2) to accomplish this with your internal customers will help you identify details that will help. As a matter of fact, when it comes to the heart of the house, sometimes the greatest product can arise from the humblest of circumstances.

For example, what do Steve Jobs of Apple, Elliot and Ruth Handler of Mattel, Walt Disney, Henry Ford, Bill Hewlett, and David Packard all have in common? Each started their large corporations—literally—in a garage. C. E. Wooman actually started what became Delta Air Lines out of a gas station garage, and DeWitt and Lila Wallace nurtured *Reader's Digest* from a garage apartment.

There's nothing special in the physical aesthetics of a garage. It's simply that it can act as a focused incubator for possibilities because it is stripped down to the bare essentials. This distraction-free environment focuses energy on the more important goals of identifying that "game-changing idea" or truly understanding the customer. The idea of working from a simple garage suggests a state of mind and a rejection of the status quo in search of the next big thing.

Obviously, you must provide people with the resources they need to do their job—everything from the right hardware and software to furnishings and tools. Ultimately, however, the crucial resource is that they are in an environment that supports the culture you want to create.

Supporting the Culture: Quality Going Down the Toilet

Today, most people know it as a company that offers sinks, toilets, bathtubs, and especially brass faucets, but the bold look of Kohler originated with immigrants from the late 1800s who excelled in European craftsmanship. To get these potential workers to come to America and accept work in its sometimes bitterly cold factory town in Wisconsin, Kohler had to invest in their entire employee experience. Now, however, guests visiting this amazing community of Kohler, Wisconsin, can stay at the American Club, which has been rated an AAA Five Diamond Award property for more than 22 consecutive years. This Tudor-style facility, which was renovated for guests staying in the area, was originally created to provide respectable housing, meals, and recreational facilities (including a bowling alley) for employees who could not afford them on their own. It's a 19th-century testimony to the idea that if you invest wisely in the experience of your employees, you will set the stage for generations to come of being able to offer a product or service that excels. If you create the right environment for your employees, they will behave in a manner that generates excellence.

Employee support takes many forms, for good or bad. Though some companies choose to have their corporate offices in key cities like New York and Tokyo, Sam Walton chose Bentonville, Arkansas, as the world headquarters of what would become the world's largest retailer, Wal-Mart. Why? Because, in part, the area provides year-round hunting and fishing for his employees. And because this was an important desire for them, this kind of decision making reinforced their culture of success.

Does your workplace support your organization's values? Take teamwork, for example. During the early days of the Walt Disney Company, artists and others would eat lunch at their desk and then go out and play touch football or softball in Griffith Park for their official lunch hour. Everyone came out and participated as a cohesive team of colleagues.

Then, when Walt Disney built the new studio in Burbank, he focused on creating a place that really supported the artists. He designed the facility so that as much natural light could be harnessed and directed as possible. This was a feature that benefited the entire team equally. But he also made a mistake by creating a space known as the Penthouse Club. This was an exclusive "members only" employee area, where the qualifying criterion was earning a certain amount of money a week. Many animators fell below the line, and resentment about this exclusionary practice became the first seeds of a labor strike that ensued not long thereafter. As the legendary animation artist Marc Davis described it: "I think the strike changed everybody. I think that Walt became resigned that he had to operate in a more hard-nosed way, like a lot of other people who have something forced on them that they don't like. I don't say that he was less benevolent. But I think that a lot of the frills that he thought were so wonderful when we first came out to the new building … went by the boards. I'm sure that he had to feel that [the strike] was a thing against him personally, and I guess in some areas it certainly was" (Thomas 1998).

Some executives understand that the workplace suggests much about the culture. For instance, some will insist on having offices in the center of the building, rather than having a corner office window, allowing everyone else to share in the view. When former JetBlue CEO David Neeleman flew, he sat in the last row of the aircraft—where the chair cannot recline. Passengers didn't recognize him, but the crew did—and the message he sent of putting the customer first was extraordinarily impressive.

The key is to visibly model your corporate values. For some leaders, the message they want to send through the workplace is the value of creativity and innovation—for example:

◆ Red Bull's London office offers slides that people can use to go between floors as well as conference room tables in the shape of ping-pong tables.

✦ Pixar's animators decided early on that they didn't want cubicles. So instead, Pixar has little cottages or huts, each of which is an office decorated in one of a variety of themes. Each has an address. Scooters are common everywhere.

✦ Borrowing on the clean-and-lean look, take a trip to the VW Phaeton Plant. There is nothing greasy, cluttered, or dirty about this plant. The physical plant is building VW cars while maintaining an environment as slick as an Apple store.

✦ When Paul Comstock, landscape imagineer for Disney, needed to build the massive savanna for the Kilimanjaro Safari at Disney's Animal Kingdom, he set up a tent as an office on the edge of the grasslands so that he could operate "out in the field."

✦ In the firm's early days, Google's employees worked at desks that amounted to wooden doors laid on two sawhorses. Offices now are high-density clusters with three or four staffers sharing spaces with couches and dogs. Recreation facilities include workout rooms, washers and dryers, a massage room, video games, and a baby grand piano. Roller hockey is played twice a week in the parking lot.

Although the tactical application varies, the message is constant and simple: Let your workplace reflect the culture you are trying to establish.

Get a Clue—for Culture

If changing your entire physical plant isn't in the budget this year, consider just working on a "culture clue," a simple reminder in the workplace that helps reinforce what you do and who you are. The simplest of these is the bulletin board. Almost every office has one near the break room. What's posted (and what isn't) on this board sends a huge message about your culture. While there, look for the trophy cabinet as well. What's the date of the organization's last accomplishment? Who and what were recognized? Is it even dusted?

Let's consider an example. At the headquarters of Southwest Airlines near Dallas, the first thing you see is a huge model airplane surrounded by tangible evidence of the pride the company has engendered in the Southwest Airlines family. Most of the huge building appears to be more museum than operational offices. Nearly every foot of wall space is covered with small, inexpensive items such as photographs, posters, inspirational quotes, recognition awards, and memorabilia spanning the company's notable history—all greeting you with the distinct message that Southwest's people are the true fuel that flies its jet fleet.

Another location for a culture clue is to go online to the home page of your company's intranet site. First, is the information current? This is a clue about the company's attention to detail and where things are going organizationally. Second, what messages are posted about the culture? Culture clues exist throughout the workplace. For instance, many people who visit the Disney theme parks around the world are familiar with the windows on Main Street USA. These windows, which bear the names of past and present Disney leaders, are the highest form of recognition Disney bestows. And the windows also remind its employees of what its culture represents—the friendly faces of people seeking to create happiness.

Culture clues offer direction and inspiration to employees internally. Many times they are embedded reminders to the employees of the service they are expected to offer. Here's another example: When was the last time you visited TGI Friday's? Did you know that in nearly every restaurant, you will find a rowing scull, along with a pair of saddle shoes and a champagne bottle placed inside? It's an internal story that's been told throughout the company for years. In fact, it's a reminder to every TGI Friday's employee about the importance of teamwork. When you go inside next time, ask any of the servers to tell you the story about the rowing scull.

On a simpler level, ?What If!—an innovative, award-winning product development company—was celebrated as Britain's happiest workplace in both 2004 and 2005. Photos of its employees across the organization adorn the walls of its boardrooms. Inside the hub, you'll find specific instances of contributions employees have made written across the walls and the ceiling. These kinds of simple, authentic gestures that align with your values make great culture clues.

Summing Up

Buckminster Fuller, a futurist and a global thinker, stated that "you can't change the people. But if you change the environment people are in, they will change." This thinking summarizes what is so important about the workplace. Externally or internally, you have an opportunity to modify your workplace to optimize your organization's brand and culture.

Next steps for building the culture through the character of your workplace:

+ What behavior do you want to change or promote in your employees? What can you do to promote this through the workplace?

+ Separate onstage from backstage areas. Invite employees to behave accordingly based on whether they are onstage or backstage.

+ Make facilities so that they are open and available to all employees. Avoid creating areas that separate or rank individuals.

+ Provide a space where employees can be creative and innovative.

+ Check your bulletin board, your trophy case, and/or your intranet home page. Are they sending the right messages about who you are? If not, make the necessary changes.

+ Is there a quotation that expresses the core of what you are as an organization? Do you have it posted where everyone can see it?

Chapter 8

Harnessing the Power of Processes

Consider these situations involving processes (P4, in the context of the World Class Excellence Model; see figure 4-1):

+ Your company laptop needs a new battery. You contact your IT department and are told that there are none in stock, but you can't find the correct bar code to order the new battery.

+ You head to the employee cafeteria where one queue exists to serve more than 150 employees coming through during the same hour.

+ When you visit the corporate office in Dayton, you need to present your corporate identification to get in. When you visit the Omaha office, you walk in without anyone asking to see any identification whatsoever.

+ Speaking of your corporate ID, you are told that you can renew that ID online, which you do. But you never get the new ID. Several calls later, you find out that they no longer have your photo on file and that you need to go over to the employee services office to get it renewed.

+ You return your company logo shirt because it's the wrong size. The employee services manager informs you that he will need to a find a manager to approve the return.

It is interesting how these frustrating scenarios sound like similar experiences we all have had as consumers in the marketplace. The reality is that employees experience many of the same challenges as external customers when it comes to processes.

Though we explore specific challenges and solutions of processes relating to external customers in part III of the book, this chapter explores them from the employee's point of view. And it also includes these processes that are unique to the employee experience:

+ Supporting employees (and customers) with effective organizational structures.
+ Giving the gift of time.
+ Providing employee choices.
+ Providing continuous employee improvement.
+ Communicating clearly with employees.
+ Learning from mistakes.
+ Busting service silos.

Let's consider how these processes can have the greatest impact as you seek to create a world-class organization.

Supporting Employees (and Customers) with Effective Organizational Structures

One of the most significant factors for the effectiveness of processes is organizational structure. The structure, combined with the culture (specifically, the informal rules that influence how people interact), will dictate what and how communication flows through the organization. The only way a company will be easy to do business with externally is if it structures itself internally for ease of doing business.

Inefficient processes within the operation will *always* affect the customer experience—by requiring more time, effort, or a higher price—due to the higher costs of the extra labor required to do inefficient processing. One example of this is from Walt Disney World. In the 1990s, George Kalogridis, then vice president of the Epcot theme park, was walking through the Land Pavilion, one of the park's largest attractions. He noticed that the fountain in the center of the building was not functioning.

Because the fountain was surrounded by the food court, he mentioned the problem to the managers of food and beverage services, but they argued that the problem was not theirs—it was the responsibility of the people responsible for attractions. When the executive requested action by the attractions managers, they too claimed that it wasn't their responsibility—it was the job of maintenance. The executive then approached the maintenance managers, who claimed that they couldn't do anything until the responsible work area filled out a work order.

It became obvious that operating in silos (these are vertically organized, isolated areas of an organization's operations led by influential people; see below for the details) left everyone only concerned about their specific duties rather than the overall excellence of the organization. In time, it was decided to change the organization into integrated business units, with each responsible for all the aspects of their unit's operations—from food to fountains to maintenance.

Part of this shift included the realignment of accountability and performance bonuses. Rather than only being rewarded on local performance, which undermined teamwork, the bonuses were balanced between the business unit and the entire park—providing an incentive for everyone to work together as part of a larger team to achieve performance excellence.

An organization's structure affects all aspects of its operations, from relationships and communication to processes and its overall personality. This structure has three key facets:

+ the chain of command
+ flattening the hierarchy
+ matrix organizations.

The chain of command, or the hierarchy, is the number of formal leadership layers in the company. Each layer is a step or filter through which a message must pass to be considered in the communication process.

Each additional step adds more time needed to address issues. In today's ever-faster-paced work environment, time/speed is a critical resource to remain competitive. Each layer also adds a filter, potentially changing or even omitting important information needed to make informed choices about the situation.

With respect to the second key facet, flattening the organizational hierarchy, the general trends for all world-class businesses over the past decade have been toward this flattening—limiting the organization to the fewest levels or layers possible. Aspects of the structure that reflect the hierarchy include job descriptions (responsibilities and authority), reporting structure (positions and accountability), and processes (general work and information flow). Flat organizations emphasize a decentralized approach to management that encourages high employee involvement in decision making. The purpose of this structure is to create independent small businesses units that can rapidly respond to customers' needs or changes in the business environment.

With respect to the third key facet, matrix organizations, more and more employees expect to be better connected with what is going on within the organization. The trend toward larger corporations has created a need to develop variations that allow for easier access to resources while maintaining more manageable access to the organization's people and processes. One such common organizational structure among world-class businesses is the matrix.

In a matrix organization, teams are formed and team members report to two or more managers. A matrix structure utilizes functional and divisional chains of command simultaneously in the same part of the organization, commonly for one-of-a-kind projects. It is used to develop a new product, to ensure the continuing success of a product to which several departments directly contribute, and/or to solve a difficult problem. By superimposing a project structure upon a functional structure, a matrix organization is formed that allows the organization to take advantage of new opportunities. This structure assigns specialists from different functional departments to work on one or more projects being led by project managers. The matrix facilitates working on concurrent projects by creating a dual chain of command—the project (program, systems, or product) manager and the functional manager. Project managers have authority over activities geared toward achieving organizational goals, while functional managers have authority over promotion decisions and performance reviews. An example would be an aerospace firm with a contract from the National Aeronautics and Space Administration.

Matrix organizations are particularly appealing to firms that want to speed up the decision-making process. However, the matrix may not allow long-term working relationships to develop. Furthermore, using multiple managers for one employee may result in confusion as to manager evaluation and accountability; thus, the matrix system may actually intensify the conflict between product and functional interests.

The balance between having enough steps and/or layers to process information efficiently and having too many steps or layers is constantly evolving. World-class organizations have found that this balance is best achieved with open and honest communication and engaged employees closest to the operational/customer situation.

Giving the Gift of Time

Giving your employees more hours in the day can be a powerful way to create greater internal satisfaction. Here are a few exemplary innovative practices that organizations—rated by *Fortune* as among the 100 best companies for which to work—are implementing for the benefit of their employees:

+ Genentech offers doggie day care and an onsite farmer's market.
+ Many firms offer health care clinics; Qualcomm's onsite primary care clinic quadrupled in size.
+ There are concierge services at Alston & Bird.
+ There is a free onsite gym at Russell Investments.
+ eBay offers golf lessons, bike repairs, a dentist, and prayer and meditation rooms.
+ Valero Energy makes its corporate jet available for employees with medical emergencies.
+ The headquarters of the pharmaceutical manufacturer Astra-Zeneca has onsite haircuts, video rentals, massages, tennis and basketball courts, and a child care facility.

Providing Employee Choices

Many employers have learned in recent years that "one size fits all" doesn't work for their employees, making the effort expensive regarding morale and loyalty. Conversely, providing relevant options can often pass on savings not only to employees but also to the employers. For example:

- Ericsson allows employees the option of bringing their pets to work.
- Principal Financial Group allows you to buy time off.
- Walt Disney World has given many of its office employees the choice of a four-day rather than five-day workweek to save on transportation and related costs.
- Despite many challenges in moving, Interaction Associates, a small consulting firm with about 100 employees, allowed them to choose the actual physical location of their new headquarters (Lorber 2008).
- Kodak invites its employees to have a say in resolving workplace disputes by inviting them to participate in a jury of their peers (Clark 2004).

Many companies urge employees to give to charities, but not all of them help make it easy to give. O2, a British mobile telephone company, has launched a program called Give As You Earn that enables employees to donate through their payroll. The process is quick and easy, encouraging employees to sign up then and there.

Analytical Graphics Incorporated doesn't just provide a flexible schedule option for its employees, many of whom work on schedules spread across all hours of the day. It actually serves three meals in its dining room and invites employees' families to come too. An in-house laundry and gym are additional choices that support the employee experience.

Clearly, there are numerous ways to give employees a greater voice in what occurs at their workplace.

Providing Continuous Employee Improvement

In the same way that employees should be continually improving the customer experience, they should also be focused on making employee workplace improvements. This shouldn't be a "program" but rather a business philosophy in any organization. Here are some examples of continuous employee improvement tactics at some *Fortune* 100 companies and other corporate organizations:

+ *On My Mind,* a blog from the Cisco CEO John Chambers, solicits employee ideas.
+ At the small business software firm of HCSS, open-book management and courses on ownership thinking led to cuts of $500,000 from the 2009 operating budget.
+ The 142-year-old textile producer Milliken has had an eightfold safety incidence rate decline since 1981, due to employees controlling the safety process.
+ SRA International, an IT consultant, asked its employees about what benefits matter most. The result was that it switched insurers, added health savings accounts and adoption aid, and increased 401(k) matches.

Imagine asking your employees for ideas on how to improve the organization—and obtaining more than 38,000 suggestions. That's what happened the first year when the Barack Obama administration launched the SAVE program, which offers federal employees the chance to submit their ideas for how government can save money and perform better. Then the program invited the public to determine a winner from the four top choices. Though the person who submitted the winning idea met the president and had her idea included in the upcoming budget, many of the other good ideas were also implemented.

The purpose of any employee-led improvement process is to see how well the company is serving its internal customers (employees), enabling effectiveness, efficiencies, and product improvements that will lead to superior external results.

Communicating Clearly with Employees

How employees communicate reflects quite a bit about the organization's health and the ability to execute excellence. The primary gauge of world-class business communication is how well the organization's values and vision are consistently reinforced.

Consider the opportunities you have for communicating and reinforcing the messages you want to permeate your organization. There are many examples that enhance communication with employees:

- ✦ Florida Hospital Celebration Health hosts a major internal event where employees can learn details about significant company activities.
- ✦ At Rackspace Managed Hosting's bimonthly open-book meetings, all financial issues are laid out for the employees.
- ✦ At Adobe, the CEO answers emails within 24 hours.
- ✦ Four times a year, Nike employees are invited to an all-employee meeting. Celebration Healthcare does similarly.
- ✦ Founder Jerry Yang at Yahoo! offers monthly Chat 'n' Chow lunches, along with answering employee questions online.
- ✦ Time Warner CEO Jeffrey L. Bewkes holds a series of lunches with 10 to 12 high performers who typically have little or no access to him. The time is spent discussing his vision and answering questions.

One of the reasons communication is so important is that it is foundational for building relationships. For instance, when Disney's Epcot theme park was being constructed, a particular engineering division of Walt Disney Imagineering, called 510, was struggling to work well with others. The artists and architects who dreamed up the rides and attractions were disappointed that the engineers in division 510 weren't living up to the earlier vision of what was to be built. Meanwhile, the construction team was angry that it was taking so long to get the blueprints delivered. A new manager, Art Frohwerk, came up with the idea of putting money into the budget for employees in the division to take others out to lunch. The condition, however, was that they had to use money to take peers at their level out for a meal.

The result was transformative. Corporate acknowledged the engineering department with T-shirts that read "I love 510" and held a celebration to honor the previously hated division. Soon, they conducted a session to analyze the progress they were experiencing. Eventually, engineering division 510 became known internally as the team that "picks up where dreams left off."

Learning from Mistakes

The story is told of a floating dormitory for oil workers in the North Sea that rolled over during the night and killed more than 100 people. Upon trying to understand why this may have occurred, it was eventually discovered that just weeks before, a crack in a support structure had been painted over instead of being reported and repaired. This small mistake caused the superstructure to fail, sinking the dormitory (Berkun 2005).

This contrasts with the standards of Granite Construction, which makes roads, bridges, and dams. Its commitment is "If you or anybody feels something is unsafe, [stop and notify someone, and] you will not be fired. You will be rewarded" (*Fortune* 2008).

Having a culture and the processes in place that allow people to report, manage, and learn from their mistakes is paramount for world-class organizations. An example from a state prison paints a clear illustration of why learning from mistakes is so imperative. One important policy for the prison's corrections officers was that "failure to do a head count will lead to termination."

The problem with using policies to run an operation is that, eventually, more effort is spent on ensuring that the policy is followed rather than operating based on why the policy was created. In this instance, some inmates started keeping track of the guards and who was doing head counts and paying attention to inmate activity and who wasn't. Eventually, two inmates broke out of the prison, causing all sorts of havoc.

The good news is that both escapees were eventually captured and returned. The press inundated the prison with reporters and media equipment. The governor, who was fairly new in office, turned to his equally new deputy of corrections. It is here that the story takes a very interesting turn. When asked for the names of who was going to be fired for the mistake, the deputy offered only his name. This deputy happened to be brand new to the role—he barely had the opportunity to visit the operation, much less provide meaningful administration. His opinion was that first-time offenses should be learning opportunities. Imagine if everyone was fired for every mistake, then no one would be open to learning—only not being caught making any kind of mistake. The true problem, according to the deputy, was that the prison had a culture of placing blame rather than correcting mistakes. The deputy's new approach transformed its results in a very short timeframe.

When employees make these kinds of mistakes, what should you teach them to do? Here are some guidelines from world-class businesses:

+ *Rule 1: Admit to it right away!* Let your manager hear about it from you first. Be proactive and seek out everyone who needs to know. Take responsibility. Don't create blame.
+ *Rule 2: Clean it up.* Do whatever is necessary to make the situation whole again for those around you. Remember, making a tighter cycle will help you to not create a problem so big that you become bogged down cleaning up after your mistakes.
+ *Rule 3: Learn from the experience.* Focus on what worked while addressing what did not work. Communicate what you have learned to others so they don't make the same mistakes. Also, learn from your challenges, but don't make them so big that they hinder your ability to move on.
+ *Rule 4: Do not take that action again.* Continue pursuing different possibilities. Keep the cycle moving. There are plenty of new potential solutions to explore.
+ *Rule 5: Regain focus—move forward.* Come back to your initial goal and continue to move forward. You can't create results if you constantly focus on what has gone wrong. But this doesn't mean that you don't learn the needed lesson. For example, it's said that a key strategy for great golfers is that they don't dwell on how they got to where they are on the green; instead, they place their entire focus on what they need to do to get the golf ball into the hole.

There's a saying: "If you hit the bull's-eye every time, then you're too close to the target." The fact is that, if you aren't making mistakes, you're not taking sufficient risks—and are likely undermining your potential. In business today, that could be the riskiest thing to do. As Bill Gates, the chairman of Microsoft has been quoted as saying, "You can tell a lot about the long-term viability of any organization by how they handle mistakes" (as quoted in Nelson 2002).

Busting Service Silos

Service silos are ineffective, vertically organized, isolated areas of an organization's operations led by influential people who are characterized by the following:

+ They avoid taking any responsibility for areas not directly under their control.
+ They expect bureaucratic processes to support their agenda.
+ They hold key information close to themselves, failing to share it with other involved parties.
+ They are quick to acquit themselves while pointing blame at others.
+ They speak in terms of "you" or "I," not "we" or "us."
+ They are obsessed with what they can control rather than with what they can influence.
+ They often act in an overbearing fashion toward others, rather than collaboratively.
+ They are frequently slow or the last to get on board with a new program.
+ They are more focused on their own interests than on what is ultimately best for the customer or the organization.

Service silos prevent an organization from creating an optimal service experience. Some have characterized the people who support these silos as cancers within an organization—caring basically only about their own well-being, to the detriment of the company. It's critical for leaders to identify ways to break down those silos and rid the workplace of these attitudes by influencing change for the better.

Summing Up

It is clear that many processes have an impact on the employee experience. Regardless of differences, every organization seeking to become world class must pay attention to those rules, policies, structures, and guidelines that support its optimal organizational culture. Processes are often the least-regarded, but usually the biggest, roadblocks to creating a successful organization. The bottom line: World-class organizations make sure that their processes make it easy for employees to do business within the company.

Next steps for building your organization's culture through efficient and effective processes:

+ How can you make waiting more bearable for employees?
+ How can you deliver service more consistently to employees?
+ How can you give the gift of time to employees?
+ How can you break up those barriers to great service?
+ What options can be given to customers to optimize their employee experience?
+ How can you continually measure and improve upon the service you provide?
+ How can you flatten your organization—or better yet, flip the hierarchy so it better supports employees serving the customer?
+ What can you do to better get the word out to employees?
+ How can we enhance working together to attain results?

Chapter 9

Providing Products That Motivate Your Employees

What would an employee consider to be the product? Just as with the external customer, the employee is also receiving goods and services. The important thing is to make sure that you are "selling" what your target (internal) customers want to "buy" (P5, product, in the context of the World Class Excellence Model; see figure 4-1). Consider their Customer Compass and your core values and vision—what do they regard as valuable? Working to consistently deliver these offerings with high quality is a very wise investment. This chapter offers several guidelines.

World-class organizations understand that the benefits and compensation packages they offer are real products that they can "sell" to their employees. When viewing the employee as an internal customer, it becomes suddenly apparent that they have similar options regarding "doing business with you"—or not. Ultimately, your employees will judge whether or not it makes good sense to remain with you or to simply stay and generate less effort.

According to the fifth annual MetLife (2007) study of employee benefits trends, employee retention is the top benefits objective among employers—edging out controlling costs for the first time since the study's inception. Employee retention was identified as the most important benefits objective by more than half (55 percent) of employers overall. Certain industries, such as retail (62 percent) and services (59 percent), were even more likely to place importance on workplace benefits as a retention strategy.

One important insight: Consider compensation and benefits as far more than the insurance packages and vacation time. Employees also "benefit" from the corporate culture in less tangible ways. Our focus here is to think of compensation and benefits in the same way you would think about the products and services you offer your external customers. In that light you want to provide to your employees a world-class product that not only attracts and keeps them, but makes them loyal and engaged with your business.

Pay

There's no question that greater pay to an employee is as attractive as the lowest price is to the consumer. To that end, *Fortune* magazine touts the 25 top-paying companies and what they do to the financial bottom line of their employees. If you are a lawyer, a nurse, or even a secretary, you can see just how much others are making. But being the highest paying company is much like being the lowest cost provider of goods and services. You will, ultimately, become a commodity—always in competition to be the top provider in terms of pay, competing with those that also want to have bragging rights. Moreover, you will tend to attract employees who feel pay is the most important aspect of their work. Do you want an employee that values money over serving your customers? Finally, what if another company tries to lure them away over price? Then you may find yourself in a no-win game of trying to retain employees chasing an ever-escalating salary—not a sustainable, or desirable, situation.

Instead, choose a better way. World-class organizations focus on developing an entire package to attract the best employees possible. This doesn't mean that they don't seriously consider salary. They simply make pay just high enough so that it doesn't become a deterrent, causing great talent to flee elsewhere. The best organizations will pay an above-average salary, but they refuse to position themselves in the highest percentile. Instead, they focus on creating a culture-based package.

Packaging Employee Benefits

The MetLife study cited above also reveals a strong correlation between benefits satisfaction and job satisfaction. Among employees who are "highly satisfied" with their benefits, 80 percent indicated strong job satisfaction, up from 65 percent in the previous year's study. Of the employees surveyed, 72 percent said workplace benefits were a reason for joining their current employer, and 83 percent said they were a factor in remaining there.

It's more than basic insurance and an annual picnic. Table 9-1 gives a variety of employee benefit offerings to be considered.

Branding Your Benefits

Some of the items mentioned above are typical. Others are more unusual. Here are some examples of non-salary-related benefits that selected world-class companies have introduced to show their care for their employees:

+ Many organizations provide child care. The Methodist Hospital System in Houston significantly subsidizes child care for any employee earning less than a certain amount.
+ Umpqua Bank, on the West Coast, allows its employees 40 hours of paid time to volunteer in the community.
+ Cornell University—ranked number 1 by AARP for best employer for workers over 50 years of age—offers a special program called Opportunities for Healthy Agencies, which targets health and fitness issues faced by older adults.
+ Starbucks offers health care for part-time employees—an important feature for people not working full time.
+ Network Appliance not only supports autism research but also provides autism benefits to its staff.
+ Google offers free meals, washing machine use, and onsite car washes and oil changes.
+ When the homebuilding industry slowed, David Weekley Homes canceled its annual reward trip and tripled severance pay for laid-off employees.

Table 9-1. Employee Offerings to Be Considered

Professional and Career Development

Corporate university: culture development, brand development, technical skills development, leadership development

Onsite learning services: library services, career resources, brown bag workshops, web and video seminars, computer-assisted learning

Higher education: onsite college courses, educational reimbursement plans

Health Care Benefits

Medical plans, prescription plans, dental plans, group life insurance, long-term care insurance

Complimentary and Discounted Offerings

Complimentary use of services and facilities, visiting retailers, discounts to local retailers, discounts on products and services, corporate retreats

Onsite Basics

Food and beverage: break rooms/kitchens, cafeteria

Personal: spa, hair stylist, day care

Corporate stores: convenience items, logo items, limited edition items

Retirement Benefits

Earnings before interest, taxes, depreciation and amortization; pension plans; employee stock purchase program; savings bond purchase plan; insurance services

Financial Services

Credit union, payroll deduction, saving accounts, flexible spending accounts, notary

Time Off/Leaves of Absence

Personal time off; sick pay, medical leave, and extended illness bank; family leave; holidays—shared and variable; vacation; jury duty; bereavement catastrophic leave; military leave

Work-Life Programs

Life-management tools: self-management, finding caregivers, parenting, special needs/disabilities, education, choosing schools and finding financial aid, caring for older relatives, preparing for parenthood/adoption

Employee Assistance Program: stress management, relationship management, crisis intervention, psychiatric counseling

Wellness programs: health fairs, walk/run events, health fairs, office gyms, self-defense programs, weight management programs, nutritional programs

Sports leagues and events: sports leagues, sports tournaments, sports trips, youth sports leagues, access to sports tickets

Clubs: service groups, environmental groups, religious organizations, diversity groups, hobby groups

+ Nordstrom offers a free notary public.
+ Microsoft matches any employee charitable contribution dollar for dollar, up to $12,000 a year.
+ Boston Consulting Group's package includes free health insurance, three months' paid maternity leave, and a bonus 15 percent of pay deposited in a retirement plan.
+ TD Industries has declared that no one at this employee-owned construction firm earns more than 10 times anyone else.
+ ChoicePoint, a LexisNexis Company, supports continuing education by offering an in-house technical "learning lab" available 24 hours a day, 7 days a week.
+ One of the first credit unions in California, 1st United Services, offers free access to a professional financial adviser.
+ Quicken loans company-sponsored bus rides to Cleveland Cavaliers games, a team owned by the company's CEO.
+ Timberland offered up to $3,000 subsidy for a hybrid car and 40 hours of paid volunteer work.
+ Senior executives at JetBlue match employee contributions to a charity fund, dollar for dollar. Typically, their entire salary is offered up in this exchange.

The primary message from these examples is that what makes a benefit great is making it valuable to your employee and unique to your culture and brand. It's one thing to match what others are offering as benefits. It's another to create benefits that really stand out in ways that align with your employees' values (what your company has in common with employees that are the "right fit"). This approach adds value to the products you offer your employees, in a way only you can provide—giving you a competitive employment edge.

The Dangers in Cutting Benefits

A common practice among corporations, particularly in difficult times, is to cheapen the products provided to employees. This shortsighted approach to your internal customers often results in severely undermining the trust and value of the working relationship.

Keep in mind the Six Ps Customer Formula (see chapter 4); the promise and the price aspects of the formula will be affected by any change in the delivery portions of the experience. Think about how external customers would react; would cheapening the product be acceptable to them? Would it affect their loyalty—and possibly your bottom line?

One way to avoid this trap is to involve your employees in the process of making any changes to their internal products. If circumstances warrant a change, sharing the details openly with the employees, and then including their suggestions will often reveal solutions you wouldn't have considered. Showing a continued commitment to the original promise and their value of the experience will generate goodwill and provide perspective for whatever action must be taken to address the situation. Ensuring buy-in during this process will allow for a seamless commitment from your employees as everyone transitions through the challenging phase.

Psychic Income

Rather than thinking about how to cut back on benefits, consider focusing on improving the mental benefits of working for you as the leader. Though, clearly, there are benefits from the status of working for a world-class organization, there's an even more influential consideration. It's been said that people don't leave companies; they leave bosses. People generally stay not because of the brick, mortar, or logo but because of the people with whom they enjoy associating and how they get to do their work. Though these benefits can't always be calculated in monetary terms, they are often measured in terms of employee engagement.

Employee engagement is a key component in the Chain Reaction of Excellence we described in chapter 1. Engagement is achieved by improving the entire culture defined by the Six Ps Customer Formula. Note how employee engagement is defined by research leaders like the Gallup Corporation. With more than 30 years of in-depth behavioral economic research involving more than 12 million employees, Gallup determined that the most critical elements of employee engagement came down to 12 core activities, known as the Q12. These statements suggest that employee engagement dramatically increases when employees understand what is expected of them, when they have the tools and resources necessary to do their job, even when they have a best friend at work. Gallup has proven quantitatively that this works, and that those who are highly engaged truly see greater results in financial performance or customer satisfaction.

The real need regarding employee engagement is best viewed in public-sector organizations. Often these employees stay with their employers for 25 years or more. If a private-sector business had customers who had been loyal for 25 or 30 years or more, they would be elated. The experience and wisdom of long-term engaged employees are invaluable to most organizations. But when disengaged, employees can be very disruptive to an organization. We refer to these disengaged employees as "ROAD" warriors—that is, retired on active duty. They are the ones who say, "Just another 7 years until I get my retirement benefits and I'm out of here!" In reality, these individuals must be reengaged or they will become toxic to the culture.

The engagement level is important. According to Gallup Consulting (2009),

✦ In average organizations, the ratio of engaged to actively disengaged employees is 1.5 to 1.

✦ In world-class organizations, the ratio of engaged to actively disengaged employees is near 8 to 1.

Clearly, there are opportunities for improvement. The product for employees may not be as tangible as it is to external customers in terms of a previously owned vehicle, a hotel room stay, or a gym membership, but it is very real, and it remains at the heart of what creates a culture. See the following case study of how Disney does it:

Case Study: The Disney Difference

It's called the "Disney Difference." As Walt Disney World grew in terms of the number of parks, resorts, and other recreational offerings, it became increasingly difficult to hire and retain employees. Furthermore, competition grew in the marketplace, bringing efforts to lure Disney employees away to work elsewhere in the community. Some employers sounded more exciting to work for, or, at least, it was something different than being with Disney, which was for years the primary employment option in town. Competitive organizations included major hotel or restaurant chains, with outstanding benefits already in place. Other competitors were simply more convenient to commute to. After all, because of Disney's geographical size, it takes considerably more effort to get to work than it does elsewhere. In fact, working in the parks required being shuttled in and out of the employee parking area to reach your workplace. Even then, Disney knew it had to compete. In the early days, the resort was so far away from anything that employees had to make great sacrifices to show up. There wasn't even a nearby gas station, so one of the first unusual benefits Walt Disney World established was an employee gas station backstage where employees could get gas at a lower than marketplace price.

Then and now, Disney does what it has to in order to compete in today's marketplace. Though Disney's pay may only be slightly above what other local businesses offer, it has created a significant compensation package known as the Disney Difference. What is the Disney Difference? Essentially it is composed of all the discounts, services, and offerings available to cast members (employees) and their families. First of these, is the ability to enjoy the parks for themselves, their family, and friends or guests (customers) for free. But beyond this, the Disney Difference is much more:

- entire booklets dedicated to discounted savings in food and merchandise not just on Disney property but in the surrounding community
- an employee-exclusive recreation area with a beach, pools, and a sports field
- a Disney VoluntEARS group with a wide array of creative community service projects
- a number of diversity resource groups that support the unique and diverse employee population
- your work costume provided to you, with options to have it cleaned and ironed for you.
- a dedicated pool and recreation area for Disney Cruise Line crew members
- several onsite day care facilities
- apartments dedicated to international and college program employees
- onsite health care facilities and a range of programs that encourage health and fitness

- reward and recognition programs that are distinctly Disney and particularly performance based
- one-of-a-kind cast member activities like the annual canoe races or Goofy's Mystery Tour competition.

Beyond this, Disney spends much effort not only communicating these benefits to existing and prospective employees, but also branding them like a Disney movie. Under the banner of the Disney Difference and with Tinkerbell serving as sort of a mascot, they aggressively seek new recruits who would be attracted to not just a job, but also an employment experience. Moreover, they keep current cast members focused on the size and scope of the benefit package, constantly communicating all the benefits that are available. The goal is to encourage employees to use their benefits as much as possible, so they feel they are getting as much extra value being a Disney cast member as possible.

The Disney Difference is far more than just what is found in the employee newsletter. Equally important is the engagement level of employees. To that end, Disney began many years ago measuring for employee engagement, recognizing that leaders were as responsible for the morale and involvement of their cast members as they were to improving the guest experience, or paying attention to the financial bottom line. Indeed, the autocratic "my way or the highway" style of leadership was no longer an effective way to create results. They had to listen to their employees and engage them in Disney's operation.

The cumulative effect is that the Disney Difference attracts and retains the kind of employees Disney wants to retain. In every one of their 3,000 job categories, retention levels are much higher than the national average. Moreover, they've retained people who largely love the heritage and offerings Disney makes to its guests, and find joy in being part of such a unique experience. Indeed, many cast members are passionate about working in such a magical place—even though they are the people who make the place magical.

Summing Up

The bottom line is that providing products that motivate your employees is about adding value, particularly value aligned with the values that are most associated with the culture of your organization. You may not be as big as Disney or have the ability to provide as wide a selection of benefits as it can for its more than 60,000 employees, but you can make your benefit package as unique as your brand. Just as leaders need to think through the products and services their brand offers, they also need to consider how they are striving to add value to their employees' experiences.

Next steps for building the culture through product:

+ How does pay factor into your entire benefits package? How do your benefits stand out from the competition?
+ Do you promote your benefits in the same way as you promote your brand?
+ Is quality or choice the most important aspect of your employee offerings?
+ How are you balancing your overhead with providing the best in benefits?
+ Is there support to make the benefits you offer available and accessible?
+ How do you go about improving benefits while maintaining their cost-effectiveness?

Chapter 10

Understanding the Real Price of Passion

Now that we've explored the initial promise made to your employees and the delivery systems of people, place, process, and product to deliver the experience to them, we need to look at whether or not it will all be worth the price they pay—P6, in the context of the World Class Excellence Model (see figure 4-1).

Organizations often talk about the price of employee turnover. Looking at the costs of hiring new employees plus the costs of training and getting them up to speed is a factor that we should not overlook. But the emphasis here is on being proactive—keeping great employees by making it worth their price. The key consideration, of course, it to ensure that they are receiving superior value at the end of the experience.

The Price Employees Pay

A few years ago, when US Airways was facing the troubling challenges of merging two airlines, it had banners made up showing a plane taking off, with the headline "Clear Skies Ahead." Below this was another statement: "Thanks to our employees and you, our customers." It's an acknowledgment that both employees and customers pay the price when an organization is facing difficult times. Unfortunately, US Airways learned the hard way that banners are not enough. Smart organizations consistently attack the challenges employees face, and work to reduce the sacrifices they make. Again, the same Six Ps Customer Formula applies, as it did earlier in this book:

$$\text{Promise} < \text{People} + \text{Place} + \text{Process} + \text{Product} > \text{Price}$$

Consider the topics we've outlined in the previous chapters:

+ compensation
+ benefits
+ a supportive work environment
+ the behaviors of those around you
+ how you are treated individually as an employee
+ how you are made to feel special/important
+ how you and others around you were selected
+ the onboarding/orientation process you went through
+ the training and development you receive
+ succession opportunities
+ the way you are rewarded and recognized
+ how much teamwork exists
+ how effective the organizational structure is
+ whether there is a culture for taking risks and learning from one's mistakes
+ how long it takes to get the answers you need
+ how much decision making is in your hands
+ how often you are waiting for others.

These are only a sample of the experiences employees receive. When it's worth the price, employees are more engaged, more committed, and more in a position to achieve results. And employees pay both tangible and intangible prices. Let's look at each type.

The Tangible Price Employees Pay

The tangible price is more physical, more quantifiable. It shows up largely in the time and effort an employee expends on the job. This factor includes both time at work and absences.

Time at Work

How much time does an employee work? If employees are in a wage-paying position, are they being compensated with overtime pay? If they are in a salaried position, are the hours justifying the compensation received? In terms of time, employees need to consider the following:

✦ working during breaks
✦ working before or after hours
✦ working on off days
✦ working while others are asleep
✦ working while others are playing—such as during holidays.

The United Services Automobile Association was a leader many years ago when it created a four-day workweek. This is much more common these days, especially given fluctuating gasoline prices, all of which adds to the price employees ultimately pay.

Absences

Time and absences from family and friends are two different issues. Some employees work a lot of overtime but do it at home. Others work a 40-hour week but pay a premium in time getting to and from work. Still others travel extensively, which creates additional absences.

The Intangible Price Employees Pay

In defining "intangible," we mean those things that aren't easily quantitatively measured. Aspects of "intangible price" include the culture, your associates, organizational performance, and the right fit.

The Culture

Are you at odds with the mission or values of your organization—feeling they do not align with the practices of the company? Is the atmosphere too formal or too controlled? People are willing to work, and even sacrifice, for organizations with which they feel aligned. This is why you'll find the crew at Southwest Airlines pitching in and helping out, especially at check-in. It also explains why their turnaround times are often less than half the industry average.

Your Associates

Are your associates great to work with? Do you pay the price of having to put up with others? How about your supervisor? Upper management as a whole? The employees who report to you? There is an intangible price related to everyone with whom you work.

Organizational Performance

Does the success of the organization matter to the bottom-line price employees are willing to pay? One survey of 321 large U.S. employers found that high-performing companies will pay, on average, 14 percent less in annual health care premiums than low-performing ones. For companies averaging 10,000 employees, that can mean an estimated savings of $15 million annually (McGraw 2008). Clearly, employees are willing to be paid less for the opportunity to work for an organization where they can be successful. On the other hand, how many times have you heard someone say, "You can't pay me enough to ever work for that place!"

The Right Fit

Are the employees doing what they love? Are they simply putting in the hours? Are they frustrated because they don't see themselves as adequate for the position, or because they feel that the position is beneath them? Given these circumstances, they may not be willing to pay the price.

An Example: The JetBlue Call Center

It's not difficult to imagine making an airline reservation and thinking that the agent with whom you are speaking is lost in a sea of cubicles, but JetBlue took a different approach to showing up at work. It found a willing workforce in Utah ready to work from home.

The advantage for JetBlue was that it could reduce office overhead while finding an educated, capable workforce at a reasonable price. After receiving initial orientation and training, agents are equipped with a home computer. They must create a dedicated workspace that helps them to be productive from their remote location. This scenario allows the 1,500 workers to process up to 35,000 customer calls a day. The most senior 25 percent are able to choose all their own shifts, and an automated system allows agents to trade shifts.

Although JetBlue made every effort to find personable, amiable agents, having people work at home does come at a price. Supervisors contact their employees every couple of days, by phone or email, in addition to standard monitoring, but working at home does not provide the kind of one-to-one contact that such personalities require. JetBlue has had to introduce a number of interactive technologies so that agents can have the opportunity to associate with each other. These technologies, placed within the context of the Six Ps Customer Formula, are summarized in table 10-1.

Despite its unique challenges, JetBlue maintains a low single-digit turnover rate compared with the rate of nearly 50 percent for call centers elsewhere. In fact, the demand to work for JetBlue is so high that the application process is only opened once a year for a 24-hour period—when JetBlue receives 1,200 to 1,400 applicants. Agents love that they can skip the travel to and from work, all the while staying close to their family and children. It's clearly a case of understanding the employee promise and creating an experience that engages agents at a price they are very willing to pay.

Table 10-1. JetBlue's Interactive Technologies in the Context of the Six Ps

P	Description
Promise	Fun, professional opportunity in a flexible, work-at-home environment
Less than ...	
People	Working virtually with people—blogging becomes the new "water cooler"
Place	Get to work at home Must provide office within your home Must live within an hour of the JetBlue University office
Process	Automated shift trading Virtual communication vehicles for associating with others Agents may bid for six- to eight-hour shifts
Product	Benefits working with a major corporation Free travel
All of which is greater than ...	
Price	Willing to work for a lesser price than found in other major call center markets

Summing Up

There are both tangible and intangible reasons to continue doing business with you as an employer. The employee decides the value of his or her employment. Listening and understanding employees' perspectives (the Customer Compass; see chapter 2) and implementing the actions that make the biggest difference to *them* will determine whether or not the "price" of doing business with you is too high or a "fair deal"—just as it is with your external customers.

Next steps for building the culture through price:

+ What intangible price do your employees pay?
+ What tangible price do your employees pay in terms of time at work or absence from others? Are there other tangible costs?
+ What price is your employee willing to pay for intangible benefits?

Part III

Leading the Brand

Chapter 11

Communicating the Promise of Your Brand

Shifting now to the external brand side of your business, you'll discover that the essential strategy is similar to your strategy with internal customers (employees). This simplified unification is the foundation of a world-class organization's competitive edge. As mentioned earlier in the book, in the context of the World Class Excellence Model (see figure 4-1), the first element of the Six Ps Customer Formula is the promise—the upfront commitment being made to the brand and to the culture. As the catalyst of the business success formula, everything that follows the promise (the delivery of the products and services) should exceed whatever is being promised. For the brand side of your business, the promise involves much more than just marketing or advertising.

Communicating the promise of your brand means any efforts made to entice external customers to purchase the products or services you offer. Though the external promise is strongly influenced by the internal culture, this chapter explores how to ensure that the promise you're making to your external customers is one that will attract them and one you can actually keep.

Most business leaders don't realize the effect that their everyday communication has on their customers and employees because the perception of employees and customers is largely an internal process.

World-class businesses are aware how their communications—including marketing and advertising—have an impact on people's behavior. Both external and internal customers make important choices—such as with whom they will do business or for whom they will work—based on this information. What sets world-class organizations apart is that they know both their customers and employees actually view these claims as personal promises.

It's human nature to take promises very personally—regardless of whether it is in a personal or professional setting. How these promises are made and kept determines the ultimate success in maintaining loyal customers and faithfully engaged employees. Failure to live up to promises can be disastrous—even if we don't know we've made them!

At the core of this promise is trust. In their book *Vitality*, Chuck Lofy and Mary Lofy (2003) define trust as a "felt sense of safety." They see it as an instinctual feeling, even a "gut" reaction. Thus "Do I trust what you claim about your product/service is the best choice for me?" is a concept that can be applied to the brand promise.

How well is your brand trusted? Trusting the integrity of your word is at the core of your promise. Once trust is legitimately *earned,* a relationship can be built that can thrive for many years. World-class organizations consistently deliver excellent products and services to optimize their promise to external customers. In this chapter, we look at these key aspects of the promise:

+ Defining the brand promise.
+ Differentiating the promise.
+ Communicating the promise.
+ Maintaining the promise.
+ Delivering the promise.

Defining the Brand Promise

The best way a brand promise can trigger the right emotional and mental response is by clearly aligning this promise with the core of who you are. What makes for an effective brand promise? Consider how well your brand aligns with your values and vision. Your brand promise should be a natural extension of the core of what you really are. Carefully avoid sending any messages that conflict with your core.

The brand promise should also connect to your target market. How does your promise support your Customer Compass? When you connect with people's essential needs, when you consistently exceed their expectations for you, then you have a powerful promise.

The goal of your brand is not to create perfect, universal appeal. Wal-Mart and McDonald's, leaders in their industries, appeal very well to certain consumers while turning off others who are a poor fit for their particular products and services. By using the Customer Compass (see chapter 2), you can convey your promise in the language with which your customers can best connect. This is particularly true as it relates to understanding the individual's felt need. One consumer may choose a Volvo because its safety record may help him or her feel more in control. Another consumer may prefer a Porsche because he or she may value status or excitement. It all comes down to that unique individual's overriding needs and wants.

World-class organizations ensure that they align their brand promise with their core and connect to the Customer Compass.

Differentiating the Promise

Product or service differentiation is vital for the success of any organization. These days, it's almost impossible to retain all the messages with which we're bombarded daily. It's important that your brand promise is able to break through that "noise" and provide a different and better experience.

Umpqua Bank is a community bank based in Oregon that started with the philosophy of treating customers as if they had known them all their lives. While other banks were trying to process customers without them even coming inside, the intent of Umpqua Bank was to make banking a personally friendly experience for everyone who came through their doors. That attitude continues to distinguish them from their competition. They provide "pleasant surprises," such as providing a computer café, local music, and even their own blend of coffee to those who come in. Many of their locations even offer after-hours activities, from financial seminars to knitting and book clubs. As part of their efforts to "befriend their community," employees receive 40 hours of paid time each year to volunteer locally.

World-class brands have very distinct "looks" that set them apart from the competition. Consider logos, for instance—when you walk into an airport, what color is associated with the different car rental companies, like National? Avis? In each case, these companies "own" their color for their industry. Consider the meaning of anything associated with making your promise (such as communication and symbols) and ensure that you connect this meaning to the reality of how you are different and better than your competition.

The first step in differentiating your promise is to be brutally honest about who you are (brand), your core competencies, and where you are going (your vision). The second step is to thoroughly understand the capabilities of your competition and how you compare. A common and critical error many organizations make is to inflate claims about their products or services. If, for example, you are not the fastest overnight delivery service in the world, do not profess to be. Bankruptcy courts are full of business owners who boasted that they were something that they were not. The natural consequences of the customers eventually finding out the truth was to stop coming—and tell all their family and friends to likewise avoid that business. Do whatever possible to uncover the truth about your strengths and weaknesses and have the courage to act—and speak—accordingly.

That said, being different for the sake of being different is not branding. Yes, you will be noticed, but not necessarily in a way that solidifies your business standing or increases customer loyalty. In short, build on the real benefits you can honestly provide.

The ongoing success of the Wii video system is a great example of parent company Nintendo effectively differentiating its promise. In a very competitive market that typically targets the teenage male gamer, Nintendo created the "Wii Would Like to Play" campaign, which targeted moms, sisters, and even grandparents instead of teenage males. By accurately identifying themselves as a home entertainment medium rather than merely a gaming system, a new generation of software has exploded with such novel applications as the Wii Fit game and Balance Board. Now, families are burning calories together rather than passively watching television. In this regard, Wii has clearly differentiated itself from the competition.

Communicating the Promise

Business owners will often delegate the branding of the company to the marketing and sales department, while they work on other "more important" operational aspects of the business. This is usually a big mistake. In the mind of every customer, marketing/sales, public relations, and community relations are connected to operations as part of their overall experience. Most *Fortune* 500 companies are where they are today because of a comprehensive, fully integrated approach to branding that helped create a seamless, unified experience, whereby operations and marketing/sales are aligned to offer a "deliverable promise" to everyone in their market—and you can do the same.

Beyond that, consider the great logos out there, like those of Coca-Cola, McDonald's, Marriott, and Disney. Great brand promises are communicated in a few words, symbols, or particular colors. The logos for these brands are connected to an explicit message the consumer receives about what that organization is promising.

Entire graphic arts books have been written to explore the psychology and practice of effective logo development. The key thing about branding is to understand that it is much more than a logo or a tagline. When done effectively, a logo represents the promise of an experience—and it acts as a conduit to deliver the message to the minds and hearts of customers.

Maintaining the Promise

Maintaining the promise involves more than creating and following corporate logo guidelines. Of course, your promise will be much more effective if all your collateral material has a consistent look and feel. This helps, over time, to build consistent brand recognition. But there's more to maintaining the promise.

Too often, in challenging times, businesses are quick to change or alter their identity in an attempt to draw new attention to their products and services. These changes to the brand confuse customers. Instead, consider how the iconic brands have used the same taglines and logo for many years—for example, Nike's "Just do it" and swoosh. One informal rule is: "When you have become tired of your logo, tagline, and branding efforts, that's about the time they are starting to sink in, and become effective, with your customers."

Media and collateral may need updating and refreshing, but keep your promise consistent at all costs. This reinforces the appropriate messages of your established brand to your key audiences. Remember, your brand is the core identity of your company. It is the sum total of every experience (marketing, collateral, product, service, and so on) that your customer has had with your company. Your brand is more important than any advertising, public relations, or direct mail campaign you will ever execute.

Delivering the Promise

World-class organizations do more than make promises. They also deliver on these promises. That's why the other five Ps have so much validity for making an organization successful. It's the integration and execution of those Ps that truly builds a great brand. That's why the promise is not just about marketing; nor should it be left to marketers alone. It's about the entire organization being clear, focused, and supportive in delivering what the consumer is being promised.

One place where this becomes readily apparent is in the automotive world. Automakers spend billions of dollars promoting their vehicles and building brand awareness, yet studies conducted by *Consumer Reports* (2008) indicate that, in terms of car brand perceptions, the Toyota and Honda brands not only ranked first and second but also greatly outdistanced any other automaker. This is no big surprise, because these same brands consistently perform well and are ranked best in their classes in matters like reliability, design, quality, and safety. World-class organizations have discovered that, when your brand aligns with the deep wants of your customers, meeting or exceeding your brand's promise leads to superior results.

Summing Up

Both big and small organizations are capable of crafting and communicating brand promises. But what separates world-class organizations is consistently delivering on their promise. Whether it is called internal branding or any other trendy name, there must be an obvious alignment between what the organization promises and the resulting ultimate experience of external customers.

Next steps for building your brand by fulfilling your promise:

✦ What promises do your customers think you have made to them? Do they trust your promises?

✦ Can you define your brand promise so that the response from your customers is instinctually positive?

✦ How do you align your promise with the core of who you are as an organization?

✦ In differentiating your promise, do you stand out from your competition? Do customers respond to what makes you different?

✦ Do you provide consistency in how you maintain the promise?

✦ How do you deliver your promise so that there is integrity between what you say and what your customers experience?

Chapter 12

Turning Your Front Line into Your Bottom Line

It is widely held that the "people" element of any organization is its most important and challenging part—and its frontline employees are its most critical "people component," P2 in the context of the World Class Excellence Model (see figure 4-1). These frontline employees, who directly serve your customers (either externally or internally), ultimately make or break the brand experience.

The brand of any company is based on the consistent experience that its external customers receive—not from executives, midlevel managers, or frontline managers but from the frontline employees who actually interact with the customers. So what can you do to create an effective front line? There are two critical ways in which customers are affected by the people who work on the front line. The first is by the service behaviors. The second is how you reach out and make your customers feel significant or special.

Customer-Focused Behaviors

It's important to clarify the frontline, customer-focused behaviors that are critical to the delivery of service. Here are some guidelines:

- Define the behavior in terms of how everyone should interact with customers, whether those customers are external or internal.
- Underscore a common look and feel for how your employees behave—such as "They are always friendly" or "They always go the extra mile."
- Shape the behaviors as an extension of your core vision and values. If you want people to be trustworthy, you need to define what behaviors will reflect trustworthiness. If you need people to treat others with respect, you should outline what behaviors demonstrate respect.
- Clearly communicate employee responsibilities and company expectations of the stated behaviors.
- Initiate behaviors that support customizing service for individual customers in unique situations.

In some companies, managers make the mistake of trying to map out all the possible behaviors their employees should demonstrate when working with customers. But this approach is flawed, for two important reasons:

1. Scripted behaviors like these tend to come across as robotic rather than genuine.
2. It is impossible to map out all potential behaviors employees should demonstrate for unlimited unforeseen future circumstances.

A good rule of thumb is a list of approximately seven behaviors. The examples that follow show how some organizations have accomplished this.

The Ritz-Carlton Three Steps of Service (Michelli 2008, 31):

1. A warm and sincere greeting. Use the guest's name.
2. Anticipation and fulfillment of each guest's needs.
3. Fond farewell. Give a warm goodbye and use the guest's name.

The Eisenhower Medical Center:

1. Smile (unless not appropriate in the situation) and introduce yourself and your role.

2. Make eye contact and greet the patients by the name they prefer. When in doubt, always use "Mr.," "Mrs.," and the like.
3. Listen to patients without interrupting them.
4. Watch for verbal and nonverbal signs that indicate the patients are not satisfied or concerned.
5. Explain to patients what is going to be happening and why.
6. Always show respect for privacy.
7. Project compassion and concern for each and every patient.
8. When patients leave, take the time to say goodbye and warmly wish them well.
9. Provide immediate service recovery if something goes wrong.

Gaylord Resorts and Hotels Service Basics:

1. Look everyone in the eye and smile.
2. Speak first and last.
3. Look sharp.
4. Know your stuff.
5. Discover and delight.
6. Make it right.

Brookfield Zoo's Service "Bee"haviors:

Bee proactive—

- Be assertively friendly.
- Take the lead—don't wait for others to approach you.
- Look for those who especially may need help.
- Anticipate what others may need and be ready to provide it or notify someone who can.

Bee attentive—

- Acknowledge everyone in the party.
- Listen carefully to what others are saying.
- Don't presuppose what others need.
- Show genuine empathy and understanding.
- Seek clarity as necessary.

Bee helpful—

- Offer options and support to those needing support.
- Don't "pass the buck" to others to solve guest challenges.
- Provide immediate service recovery.
- Be informative and provide accurate information. Be honest if you don't know the answer, and, if possible, get the right answer.

Bee polite—

- Use common courtesies, like "please" and "thank you."
- Wait for others to finish before speaking.
- Call others by their name whenever you know it.
- Use guest-appropriate language.

Bee professional—

- Dress and act professionally.
- Wear a name tag.
- Use appropriate terms.
- Maintain a neat appearance.
- Think through your nonverbal gestures.
- Refrain from speaking negatively at any cost.
- Don't talk about business, company politics, or personal issues in front of the guests.

For decades, the Walt Disney Company listed seven key service behaviors (Cockerell 2008, 127–28) that everyone was responsible for executing:

1. Make eye contact and smile.
2. Greet and welcome each and every guest.
3. Seek out guest contact.
4. Provide immediate service recovery.
5. Display appropriate body language at all times.
6. Preserve the "magical" guest experience.
7. Thank each and every guest.

Today, Disney has updated its guidelines to the "Disney Basics," based on discussions with its guests (customers) and cast members (employees). As before, these behaviors are posted in backstage areas throughout the parks, resorts, and even cruise ships worldwide. Though based on the original seven foundational behaviors, they have been condensed to four:

1. Project a positive image (smiling, looking approachable, modeling Disney).
2. Be respectful and courteous (eye contact, greet and thank, engage children).
3. Play the part (preserve the magic, excellent quality, reduce hassles).
4. Go over and beyond (anticipate, surprise, and provide service recovery).

These behavioral basics are nonnegotiable for everyone employed by Disney—leaders as well. In fact, the leaders are responsible for these behaviors as well as additional behaviors (see chapter 6). One way to ensure that your front line is consistently providing on-brand behaviors is to provide common guidelines that are meant to be universally utilized.

Again, the point is to provide a framework that aligns behaviors while retaining the freedom within this framework to behave appropriately for whatever situation the individual encounters.

Individualizing Customer Service

Henri Landwirth was a hotelier in Central Florida. Years ago, he received a request from a family with a little girl named Amy, who had leukemia, and whose only wish was to come to Orlando to visit Disney World and the other theme parks. In wanting to do something nice for Amy, Henri quickly made arrangements to have the girl stay at his hotel. Sadly, the remainder of Amy's travel plans took too long to organize and Amy passed away before her wish could be granted.

That unfulfilled promise made Henri determined that no terminally ill child ever wanting to visit the Central Florida attractions would ever be disappointed again. So he created Give Kids the World Village, a 70-acre resort complete with villa accommodations designed for those with special needs, along with a host of entertainment attractions, whimsical venues, and recreational activities. Since 1989, about 100,000 families have been welcomed through the gates of Give Kids the World.

Doing something special for someone else is at the core of customer service. You hear those stories all the time, and it is why people grow loyal to organizations. Henri did not only seek to do something wonderful for Amy; he orchestrated something even larger that guarantees something special and wonderful for all those families with terminally ill children in need.

People want to feel special. To achieve "feeling special" requires a "special effort," particularly when numerous employees or functions are involved. World-class organizations understand this. Therefore, with over-and-above service behavior guidelines, they purposefully design experiences to make people feel special. In his best-selling book *The*

Encore Effect, Mark Sanborn (2008) describes legendary service as creating a "performance" that gets your customers buzzing. To create this effect, he suggests that when you focus on the happiness of others before your own, you will have a positive impact on them. And because people tend to want to repeat experiences that make them feel good (and tell others), you generate more business.

There are two ways in which you can make customer experiences truly unique and memorable with large volumes of unique customers that may frequent your business: choreographed care and service improvisation.

Choreographed Care

Choreographed care involves carefully orchestrated opportunities to individualize the customer experience—through planned, scheduled ways in which special service attention can be shown, for instance, the treasure box in the dentist's office.

Build-a-Bear is more than a retail store. It epitomizes choreographed care. It's entirely dedicated to making the purchase of a teddy bear a completely memorable experience. Not only are you led through the process individually by a store attendant, but you are escorted through a ceremony that brings the bear to life and makes that bear your very own.

Do you remember Farrell's Ice Cream Parlour? One of the signature events there was when you purchased a Zoo (an open silver bowl with dozens of ice cream scoops, toppings, whip cream, nuts, cherries, and small plastic zoo animals). When delivering this concoction, the staff would run around the restaurant with sirens blazing, drums banging, and lights turning on and off. Another memorable moment was when you finished eating the Pig's Trough (an individualized huge portion of ice cream). They gathered everyone's attention near you and presented a ribbon announcing the fact that you ate the entire portion.

At the Harley-Davidson Historic Factory Dealership in Orlando, they ring the bell whenever a new customer purchases a motorcycle. At Pick 'n' Pay, a grocery store chain in South Africa, the employees ring a bell whenever a fellow employee has gone out of his or her way to do something nice for someone else. They also note the deed in a large journal that sits on the podium near the bell. Here are some additional examples of choreographed care:

✦ "guest of the day" programs
✦ honorary titles, badges, and certificates
✦ honorary roles in shows, demonstrations, and events
✦ hands-on activities unique to the location
✦ special games and activities for the children
✦ opportunities to pay attention and celebrate employees.

Service Improvisation

These are "spontaneous" experiences that you provide when opportunities arise, and the best companies *create* opportunities. Service improvisation is a tool for the staff that gives it license to get creative and individualize customer service—and even become service heroes.

Service improvisation can be proactive or reactive. From a proactive perspective, it can take the form of going out and greeting customers as they are coming into your place of business. From a reactive view, it can simply be offering to take a picture of a customer. Simply put, service improvisation is a chance to do something nice for someone else that is unexpected and a pleasant surprise worth talking about. Here are some examples:

✦ A child drops an ice cream cone at a park and a worker replaces it for free.
✦ A hotel clerk notices a weary traveler and provides an unexpected upgrade for free.
✦ A car service shop brings the fixed car to the owner because of her difficult schedule.

Summing Up

When providing choreographed care and service improvisation, there are certain principles to keep in mind:

✦ Keep the individual's Customer Compass (see chapter 2) in mind when determining whether or how to best interact with the individual.
✦ Establish a good balance between being improvisational and orchestrated.

- Create low-cost or no-cost experiences for connecting one-to-one with customers.
- Provide rewards to employees who come up with low-cost and no-cost experiences that exceed the customer's expectations (and generate loyalty and advocacy).
- Consider how you can individualize service for employees (internal customers) as well.

Supporting People in Building the Brand

Because the frontline employees are so important to the brand experience, many organizations look for ways they can "fix" the customer service their frontline staff delivers. They want to make their employees friendlier or more hospitable. Their concern is that their employees don't smile enough or don't use such pleasantries as "please' or "thank you." The concepts presented above address this.

When handling behavioral shortcomings, be sure to consider other possible causes as well. Two factors commonly undermine the effectiveness of the people component.

The first factor can be found in the other Ps that support the brand. For instance, if a particular policy (process) negates the customer experience, it doesn't matter how friendly the employee is—simply saying "Sorry, I can't help you ... have a nice day" won't fix it. The real problem that creates the poor customer experience is in the process, not in the people.

The second common cause of why employee behavior fails is because of the culture itself. If you aren't providing a great internal customer (employee) experience, then it's difficult to sustainably maintain a great external customer experience. The chapters in part II on creating the culture reveal how to improve the employee experience.

Next steps for building the brand through people:

+ How do you greet your customers?
+ What are your service guidelines? How are they customized to fit your organization?
+ Do you currently provide choreographed care options? Are there activities like this from the past that you could adapt? Are there new opportunities to be created?
+ What would be the benefits of initiating service improvisation on a consistent basis?
+ How can you keep choreographed care and service improvisation fresh and alive day to day?

Chapter 13

Creating a Workplace That Strengthens Customer Service

The workplace is usually a physical setting, like a store or an office building—a place, P3, in the context of the World Class Excellence Model (see figure 4-1). It also includes the grounds around that building—the parking lot, the directional signage, and so forth. Though the obvious workplace is physical, some are virtual locations. Waiting on the phone line for an operator to transfer your call is an example of a virtual setting. Finding out the hours of operation on a website is another example of a virtual workplace. The working environment can be dedicated to the external customers, the internal customers, or both. The important thing is ensuring that your workplace serves to enhance the experience.

This chapter explores what your workplace communicates about the service you deliver. We explore how to maintain the experience as well as the concepts of "onstage" or "front of the house" as well as the "backstage" or "back" or "heart" of the house.

Does It Really Matter That Much?

A skeptical vice president of nursing for a medical center's oncology (cancer) operation once felt that its work setting was unimportant—claiming that "our patients don't care about anything other than getting better." But after accepting the challenge to experience their process by "walking in the shoes of her patients," she sat in her waiting room (doing paperwork) for the duration of the typical waiting time for the patients at that facility.

Although the chairs were sufficiently comfortable, the hospital executive noticed something while watching a family waiting for their son to go through that week's treatment: The plants lining the ceiling in the room were dying. As this family was facing a critical life-and-death scenario, the sickly condition of the plants in the room sent a disturbing message—one that certainly did not inspire the confidence and optimism desired to support the healing process.

Engage the Five Senses—Make "Sense" to Your Customers

All five of our senses—sight, sound, smell, touch, and taste—determine how we perceive our environment. Any experience, such as a traditional holiday dinner, is given meaning by our values and our senses: the smell of dinner cooking, the sound of holiday music, the taste of freshly baked desserts, and more.

Our five senses are distinctly linked to memory and emotion. If we want our customers to remember us and have an emotional connection beyond that of our competition, we must consider how our offerings affect the customer's senses and work to optimize the use of those opportunities. Let's consider each sense.

Sight

Sight is the most obvious sense on which business professionals focus. When you enter a location, you know immediately—by the way it looks—whether it is a formal or informal workplace, or a high-quality or low-quality workplace, just by viewing the carpet, the furniture, the paint, the lighting, and so forth. Similarly, when creating a cake for a wedding reception, a bakery chef will take as much care with the presentation of the cake as with the taste.

Consider the impact of not attending to even seemingly minor details. What if you were boarding a passenger jet on a major airline and, as you were walking back toward your seat, you notice that one of the windows had the trim held up with duct tape. An experienced flier might even rationalize that the inside plastic window wasn't important for safety reasons—that the exterior glass was the critical component. However, even the most logical person will eventually start to think: If their attention to detail is so poor with this "onstage" situation (were external customers will experience it), then I wonder what their attention to detail is like for the maintenance crew, or some other aspect of the "backstage" operation that I cannot see. When customers are given reasons to wonder about the unseen aspects of their experience, their trust will decrease, their imagination will begin to fear the worst, and your brand will suffer.

Clearly, what we see can have a powerful effect on our choices. Go into a grocery store and you will often find meat products packaged against green paper. The color green helps to pop out the red in the meat, making the choice more appetizing. Color and visual stimuli do much to set the sense of place.

Sound

The second sense most commonly attended to by companies is sound. Music and other sounds play an amazing role in how we respond to place.

During the last two decades, restaurants, retail stores, and hotels have become more aware of the power of sound in their customer environments. Multiple research studies have indicated that sounds have a definite impact on the behaviors of customers—for example:

- ✦ Launching a computer you hear the familiar tones of a Mac, or the AOL voice, "You've got mail."
- ✦ Nokia's ringtone is strongly associated with its brand.
- ✦ Attending to what is known as auditory stimulus, Kellogg's actually tests the sound quality when you crunch on cereal.
- ✦ For most, a revving engine has no distinguishing qualities. But a "hog" owner knows when a Harley-Davidson engine is revving up by its trademarked rumbling sound.

Hospitals and health care providers in particular are becoming more aware of this. For example, Clarian Health Partners in Indianapolis recently began providing iPods to oncology and transplant patients to keep them informed on their progress, because it reduces their anxiety and helps with their recovery. Beyond music, the clinic put in a Macintosh-based video studio and editing suite to produce an iPod program that has surgeons answering questions, gives new patients a virtual tour of the clinic, and tells individuals about their progress. Patients get tips on diet, food shopping, and exercise, as well as motivational messages. And, at the end of their stay, they get to keep the iPod and the music they also have loaded on it (Pyke 2004).

Smell

When was the last time you asked the question "What does it smell like to do business with us?" As odd as this statement is, world-class organizations include this aspect of their customer's experience when addressing operational decisions.

Remember the smell when you opened that package of Crayola crayons? That smell is patented to prevent competitors from replicating it. The average human being can recognize up to 10,000 separate odors. Smells also retain an uncanny connection to memory. A whiff of pipe tobacco, a particular perfume, or a long-forgotten scent can instantly conjure up scenes and emotions from the past.

As Starwood Hotels recently relaunched a brand awareness campaign with their properties, they knew they would need to involve the senses in defining the look and feel. This is carried out with scented candles at their Westin properties, and with fresh-baked apple pies at the Four Points by Sheraton properties. They know that the aroma is part of what creates the brand.

Walt Disney's imagineers get the concept of smell. They developed a device known as the "Smellitzer," an atomizer-like machine capable of delivering smell on cue at given locations. It's one of the reasons that attractions like "Soaring Over California," with its citrus aromas, or "It's Tough to Be a Bug," with it's stink bug smell, have been so popular. It also plays to the bottom line. Guests walking down Main Street USA at the Magic Kingdom will often stop and smell freshly baked chocolate chip cookies coming out of the bakery. The reality is that the cookies are not baked there—they are shipped from offsite. The aroma is what makes you stop and want to sample what's there. It's not even the smell of chocolate chips that brings you in—chocolate has no aroma. Rather, it's the vanilla that is being pumped by the Smellitzer into the air.

In the United States and the European Union member nations, smells can actually be trademarked if they have a "distinctive character." A Dutch perfume company trademarked the smell of "freshly cut grass" to give their tennis balls that special aroma. According to a French court, "The olfactory memory is probably the most reliable memory that humans possess. Consequently, economic operations have a clear interest in using olfactory signs in identifying their goods." Yes, focusing on what your customer smells is an awkward consideration, but it is one that makes a difference for world-class companies—and their bottom line—every day.

Touch

From birth, people crave the sense of touch. Research shows that babies can distinguish some textures right from birth. That's one of the reasons they love to be rocked. And it also helps explain why massage and spa businesses have soared in recent years. If your customers sit in a chair during their experience with you, what does that chair feel like to them? Does it set you apart from your competition? Does it add value to their experience?

Have you considered how important it is to the clothes shopping experience to physically try on the clothing? There is something incomparable about experiencing the feel and fit. Some retail experts contend that clothing will never sell as well online as it does in a retail outlet, because the tactile part of the experience is missing. The same applies to consumer activities like test driving a car. The sense of touch is enhanced as we get behind the wheel of a car and actually feel the road during the driving experience.

Considering the environment you are delivering should include asking questions related to the experience your customer is having. Examining a restaurant, for example, from the customer's perspective by asking "How thick is the chowder I'm stirring?" or "How tough is the steak I'm cutting?" can lead to enhancing the overall dining experience. Where museums historically would emphasize "Don't touch" now there is a trend to creating a much more hands-on, interactive experience. And of course, the experience of an iPhone or other hands-on products is judged significantly by the tactile experience we have with them.

Taste

In every culture around the world, people use food as a "social lubricant." When people are out in the world as consumers, it is often with others as part of a shared experience. Introducing the element of taste into your process may provide an additional connection between you and your customer.

Notice how some banks offer lollipops for children, or dog treats for pets along for the ride. These are clearly not essential parts of the banking experience, but they add that "little something extra" that sets them apart from the other banks.

Consider the discussion that occurs regarding someone's stay at a hospital. Other than the obvious—"How is your recovery?"—the most-discussed issue often centers on the quality of the hospital food. Regardless of the many different facets of the overall experience, something as (seemingly) insignificant as food becomes a very important consideration in the overall experience of the patient—and, therefore, one that must be addressed to be competitive.

Everything Communicates

Everything in the workplace is like a billboard—it advertises a message about the quality of what you do. Give Kids the World, the charitable organization in Orlando described in chapter 12, has created a beautiful place to reassure terminally ill children and the families that accompany them. Everything in the environment is designed to immerse the visitors in a fun, carefree experiences—away from the stress and heartache they typically face back home. Guests and their families step into the House of Hearts to register. From there, they go to the Castle of Miracles, the Ice Cream Palace, the Gingerbread Courtyard, and Marc's DinoPutt. It's all whimsical, but it stands as a testament that by paying attention to your facilities, furnishings, railings, landscaping, walkways, and signage, you can transform the experience for those who are in the midst of monumental struggles.

Give Kids the World follows the way of thinking that world-class organizations have mastered. Walt Disney knew that Disneyland had to be a different place than the carnivals of the day. Think about it: What do burned-out lights on a Tilt-a-Whirl sign suggest about the rest of the experience? It's no wonder that Disney pays attention to "non–theme park ride" details such as light fixtures, trash receptacles, and landscaping—and anticipates problems to those issues. Dead flowers onstage? Disney thinks ahead, and backup flowers are ready only a few yards away, in the backstage area. Some short-term flowers are often planted while still in their containers to save time and effort—they just throw on a little topsoil and they're on with the show. See the following case study of how everything communicates.

Case Study: Florida Hospital Celebration Health

One powerful example of understanding how everything communicates, especially by paying attention to the senses, comes from Seaside Imaging at Florida Hospital Celebration Health. Experts know that receiving an imaging experience can be a very stressful time. Celebration Health wanted to make imaging as easy as a day at the beach.

When you walk into this section of the hospital, the environment is completely transformed. Gone is the traditional hospital look. You hear the sounds of the beach. You smell coconut suntan oil. The hallway flooring looks like a wooden beachfront boardwalk. To change into hospital garb for the procedure, patients enter into individual beach cabanas to change into, not hospital gowns, but surfer shorts, a top, and a terry robe. They can wait their turn in Adirondack chairs, or listen to soothing ocean sounds.

For those who are particularly nervous, like children, Celebration Health has created a special area where an animatronic bear named Buddy explains the process in a calming manner. Buddy is especially designed to help adults and children understand their imaging experience while entertaining them at the same time. To top it off, the massive imaging equipment that surrounds the patient has been designed to resemble a large sand castle. You simply rest "on the beach" while listening to the sound of ocean waves and the smell of fresh ocean spray.

The results? The imaging center's adult patient sedation rate dropped from 6 to 2 percent, and cancellations were cut by 50 percent. Where technologists would previously spend 30 to 40 minutes coaxing a patient through a test, that time has been reduced dramatically. Patient satisfaction scores have improved—as well as bottom-line results. Leading with your customers can make the difference between ordinary and extraordinary! (Robinson 2010)

Rule 137: Less Is More

Have you ever been to a public pool or water park? Typically, the owners and operators of these facilities are extremely concerned about the signage. Every slide and/or pool often has a sign indicating the rules of that attraction. The rule of thumb is: Think of anything that a patron could do to get into trouble, and list it as a warning on the sign. Inevitably, signs list nearly a dozen subpoints of do's and don'ts. They read like a legal contract before swimming: 16 rules for the pool, and another 8 to 10 for the diving board. Why not 137 rules? Who reads the rules anyway? Surely not the kids who are always being warned by the whistle-blowing lifeguards!

World-class businesses have found that when it comes to rules, less is more—as at your local Apple store. Everything about the experience is notably clean, with no excess signage. An Apple store isn't like a big-box retailer with product stacked up to the ceiling. That kind of place wouldn't align with their brand. Products are displayed welcomingly, with lots of space for people to move in and play around with products.

The result: According to *Fortune* magazine (2007), Apple stores have won the title for "most sales per square foot of retail space" (more than $4,000) of any other major retail operation. An easy assumption is that it is because of all those small iPods and expensive computers. Well, consider that the title for second-highest sales is held by Tiffany & Company, which sells even smaller and even more expensive items—it earned about $2,600 per square foot of retail floor space. In a more comparable category was Best Buy, also known for high-volume electronic sales, but only earning about $930 per square foot.

In the retail industry, an important consideration is how a store displays its merchandise. Note the distinct differences between how Wal-Mart displays tons of bulk product on the shelves and how a store like Nordstrom prides itself on having its floor showcases display minimal product. Each has a strategic reason for its decision that aptly supports its brand and culture. The important—and sustainable—focus must be on creating the experience that sets you apart.

"If You've Got Time to Lean, You've Got Time to Clean"

"If you've got time to lean, you've got time to clean" was the motto of Ray Kroc, the founder of McDonald's, who built an empire based on establishing a consistent setting and product on which customers could rely. Simply said, cleanliness was so important that every spare (non-customer-serving) moment should be invested in keeping the restaurant clean.

For years, a leading car rental company followed a rigorous effort to maintain clean cars for its customers. Keeping the car clean for the next driver was an obvious requirement. However, there was an unexplained discrepancy between the excellent condition of the very clean car and the less-than-excellent perception of their customers. To solve this puzzle, the company began a detailed analysis. It discovered that its customers' overall perception of the car's cleanliness was influenced by the questionable cleanliness of its check-in counters—the customer's first impression. When the company began to improve its check-in counters' appearance, the customer's perception of cleanliness went up dramatically for the entire car rental experience. That simple adjustment improved not only cleanliness scores but also satisfaction levels and led to a positive shift in loyalty and repeat business.

The workplace plays a significant role in the perception of value for the customer's investment of time, effort, and money. Leveraging the workplace to add value to your customers' experiences will serve as a very valuable tool in building your very own world-class brand.

Next steps for building the brand through the workplace:

+ Walk in the customer's shoes of your own area, focusing on each sense.
+ Physically change the environment to juxtapose any negative stereotypes typically made of your product or service.
+ Walk around a mall or a similar operation. From simply passing by, observe what attracts you to enter or repels you from entering. Replicate what works for your business.
+ Simplify the customer space. Remove all clutter.
+ Simplify the signage. Vow that you will never put up a handwritten sign in front of external customers.
+ Measure how effective you are in consistently keeping the customer experience clean and tidy.
+ How can you model the adage "Everyone picks up trash!"?

Chapter 14

Making an Impact through Processes

Consider these situations, each in the realm of process—P4, in the context of the World Class Excellence Model (see figure 4-1):

+ A chainsaw needs a replacement part. In visiting a local home improvement store, you find out that there are none in stock, and you can't find the correct bar code for ordering the new part.

+ At a banquet, there is one line to serve more than 150 guests. With a little forethought, that same banquet table could be reorganized to accommodate two lines—and more guests at a time.

+ Standing in line at the movie theater, you find out you need to present your child's ID to get a student discount. Stepping aside to the kiosk, you find that you can purchase tickets without proof of age.

+ You thought you could renew your driver's license online. But you never received a license in the mail. Several calls later, you find out that they no longer have your photo on file and that you need to go in to have a photo taken to get the license renewed.

+ You return a gift given to you in the wrong size. The store clerk sends you to the customer service department, who proceeds to find a manager to approve the return, followed by a requirement to fill out a form with personal information—all to receive the store credit.

Each of these situations represents a process problem. The return example emphasizes the impact that processes can have on the customer experience. The store may be very trendy and its product line may be of high quality, and the store clerk may be friendly and the store may be well marketed—but all that is undermined by the hassle of simply returning an item purchased at the store.

How might a similar return situation be handled at a world-class retail organization—like Nordstrom? Customers are advocates for the Nordstrom brand. Shoppers are loyal. The product line is upscale, and the facility trendy. Despite all this, what is the best-known story told about this world-class retail chain? It isn't about its products—it is about its service. Nordstrom may be best known for the story about how a customer once brought in a tire, and, without hesitation, the store clerk provided an immediate refund. Not only was there no manager approval required, but Nordstrom, a retail clothing and housewares store, has never sold tires. (The little-known "story behind the story" is that the customer was confused because the business previously at that location actually sold the tire.) How many millions of dollars worth of word-of-mouth advertising has that single action provided for Nordstrom? And all because Nordstrom understands the importance of having streamlined processes that enhance its customers' experiences.

Processes have an impact on the service experience perhaps more than many of the other six Ps of the World Class Excellence Model. Processes are the policies, procedures, initiatives, and guidelines for delivering excellence. Any time you hear a customer say the word "hassle" when referring to doing business with you, you have a process problem. Though many processes can challenge any organization, these are some of the biggest opportunities in delivering the brand to the customer:

+ requesting information once
+ decreasing waiting time
+ giving the gift of time

✦ providing customer choices
✦ offering one-stop solutions
✦ providing continuous improvement.

Let's consider each one.

Requesting Information Once

Let's consider two scenarios:

1. You're in an emergency room. It's not life threatening, but you're very uncomfortable and you want service. While you're waiting, you're asked to complete some paperwork. The forms ask for personal information, such as name, address, phone numbers, and type of problem. You complete the paperwork as requested. By the time you're admitted, cared for, discharged, billed, and get follow-up, you have repeatedly provided that same personal information half a dozen times. Why do you need to repeat that effort so many times? From your perspective as a patient, it appears that the different hospital departments don't communicate with each other. Shouldn't there be a better solution to this common situation?

2. You need to make changes to your airline reservation. You call, and you are asked to type in your frequent flyer number. You're transferred to an operator, who then again asks for that same frequent flyer number. Why did you have to type it the first time?

Typically, the cause of this process error is because the organization views the situation from its corporate position, rather than from the perspective of the patient's or customer's experience. What would be a world-class solution? If you're asking a customer to provide you with information, create the processes necessary to populate that information across the necessary IT or other data-gathering solutions so the customer isn't troubled for that information again. With today's technology options, it shouldn't be too difficult to identify creative ways to "ask once and distribute." You'll see this kind of solution in such convenient online systems as Amazon or eBay, where once you've created an account, you don't have to explain who you are or add information every time you log in.

Decreasing Waiting Time

Most people hate waiting in line. What can you do as a service provider to remove the hassle of queuing? Though you may not be able to remove the need for waiting in line completely (for example, at a Disney theme park), you can affect the *perception* of waiting time. Here are some factors and solutions.

Shorten or Eliminate the Wait

Every day, more technological solutions are developed that remove or reduce the need to wait in line. Florida's Department of Transportation joined many highway systems across the country to provide SunPass, an electronic toll transmitter that allows motorists to bypass having to wait in line at toll booths.

For years, the managers of Disneyland and Walt Disney World focused on building rides and attractions that would maximize capacity and move park guests through more efficiently, thus reducing the wait in line. When they decided to create solutions from the guest's perspective, they came up with a technical breakthrough called FASTPASS, which revolutionized the theme park queue process by allowing guests to wait in line virtually. Guests obtain a ticket to return to an attraction at a later time, when they are allowed to walk directly to the front of the line.

Retail chains like Wal-Mart and Home Depot have introduced self-service cash registers at many of their locations. In addition to providing another option for customers, these registers provide benefits to the company as well, including reduced staff and increased store capacity.

Entertain Them

Have you ever noticed how people who are waiting in line at the grocery store peruse the magazine rack? Years ago, it was Muzak, filling silent elevator or office time with music; now it is digital displays, informing and entertaining. Have you ever filled out the required paperwork while waiting for your appointment at the dentist's office? Strategically occupying the customer's time is now accomplished in many ways.

These days, many gas stations provide video screens that play infomercials at the inside counter and at the pumps to take your mind off waiting. Phillips 76 has added an innovative low-technology—but very entertaining—distraction in the form of a children's guide to splattered bugs. Using this poster, you can tell what the dead bug on your windshield is. Done in a humorous style, moths, ladybugs, and dragonflies are included with pictures suggesting what the bug would look like smashed on a windshield. Not only do these entertaining tactics effectively occupy your time, they distract you from the cost of the gas going into your car. Optimizing the customer's waiting time is a big opportunity to improve both the customer's experience and your company's business results.

JetBlue allows its passengers to sit back at 35,000 feet and surf through 36 free channels of television programming. At Shell Oil stations, you'll find video screens that play infomercials to take your mind off waiting (not to mention the cost of pumping gas). Not only do these tactics effectively occupy your time, but they can also be utilized as a sales opportunity. Optimizing the customer's waiting time is a big opportunity to improve both the customer's experience and the company's business results.

Reduce the Anxiety of Waiting

No one likes the uncertainty of waiting. As children, we ask these questions out loud: "How long before we get there?" "Are we there yet?" As adults, we're usually still thinking them.

FedEx succeeds in part because its customers can go online any time to see the status of their package and relieve that anxiety of not knowing.

Why not reduce the anxiety of staying as well as the anxiety of waiting? No one likes the anxiety of a hospital stay, but before you check in to the Kaiser Permanente Roseville Medical Center you can watch a welcome video online (Robert Wood Johnson Foundation, 2008). Here, relevant issues concerning security, patient visits, and dispensing medications are made clear to patients.

Provide Certainty or an Explanation If Possible

The principle of providing certainty or explanation where possible works well when on hold waiting for "the next available call center attendant."

Customers appreciate it when the system provides an estimate of waiting time so they can anticipate when their call will be answered. Minimally, the recorded outgoing message should explain the delay (high call volume and the like). Even websites are seeing the value in providing a visible scroll bar being filled in while waiting for the next web page to appear, helping to provide some certainty that the system is working.

Make Waiting as Equitable as Possible

When customers perceive that their wait is longer than someone else's, they become very impatient and irritable. That's why "cutting" in line angers so many. Instead, create a process that doesn't reward circumventing the established queue. Walt Disney Attractions addressed the issue of some park guests "borrowing" a wheelchair to move directly to the front of the line. To prevent this abuse of the system, Disney changed the process. Now they make queuing aisle wide enough to accommodate park guests with wheelchairs, so everyone in a wheelchair party can progress through the line together.

It is understandable why people get angry when circumstances don't seem fair. Over the years, some businesses have created ways to make waiting as fair as possible. The system of taking a number to be served by the butcher or baker is a process that's been around a very long time. Another is being told while on hold that your call will be answered in the order it was received. Processes like these serve to help us feel that we're being treated fairly.

Let Others Wait with Them

Interacting with another individual can be a good solution for occupying time. It is also a great way to share any anxiety as it occurs. Hospital waiting rooms are an obvious example of why it's better to wait with someone you care for, rather than being by yourself. Remember when the dad-to-be used to wait it out while mom had the baby? Now sofa beds are often placed in the room with mom-to-be in case dad gets tired. Now, couples have a completely different, shared experience when their baby is born. The difference is the benefit of having access to loved ones during a time of uncertainty or anxiety—or long waiting times.

Make It Worth the Wait

Ultimately, whatever inconvenience is allowed as part of your customers' experience must be made up by you in terms of the value of your product or service. There are millions of iPhone fans who are willing to camp out in front of an Apple store to buy one, as if they were getting tickets to see their favorite rock band. The reason for this is simple: The more valuable the product or service, the more worthwhile the wait, from the customer's perspective. The trick is that this is a constantly moving target. Your customers' expectation of your experience will continue to go up, so your efforts to improve must never stop.

In summary, consider the occasions when your customers have to wait. Reduce the pain of waiting in as many ways possible to ensure that the customer's waiting investment is worth it.

Giving the Gift of Time

We live in an era when time is a premium resource. People today are willing to pay for goods and services they wouldn't have even considered paying for two decades ago because they think it will provide them with more time to participate in other (more valued) experiences. Consider these examples:

+ People will pay others (particularly in large metropolitan areas) to walk their dog because they don't have the time to do it themselves.

+ Increasing numbers of people report not cooking at home anymore. Those who do still place convenience at a premium. Companies like Stouffers have become more popular, based largely on people wanting hot meals without the hassle of cooking it themselves. In many urban areas, you can actually order groceries online or over the phone and have them delivered to your home—all to reduce the hassle of having to go out and shop.

+ People use valet services to park their car. They simply don't want to waste time trying to find a parking space and walk to and from their car.

Providing Customers with Choices

One of the best things you can do for customers is to provide them viable options. Empowering customers with informed choices gives them the power to influence their situation. For instance, consider the following:

+ Identifying a variety of ways to receive communication/information.
+ Providing a range of payment options.
+ Identifying primary, secondary, and tertiary points of contact for resolving concerns/questions.
+ Creating options for fulfilling compliance requirements.
+ Providing options in lieu of waiting on the receipt of products and services.
+ Providing more convenient options for a higher fee.

You have an opportunity to help your customers participate in the process by informing them about the available options. Open and honest information is a benefit for everyone involved. It enhances the customer experience, usually costs the business very little to provide, and serves to emphasize all the potential value the situation has to offer.

When you enter the Disney parks, you come to what's referred as a "tip board." It provides current wait times to the attractions, so you don't have to walk from one end of the park to another to learn how long the line is. You can decide immediately if you want to walk in the direction of Big Thunder Mountain in Frontierland, or toward Space Mountain in Tomorrowland.

Next, let's look at some of the many ways in which you can empower your customers and add value to the entire experience.

Offering One-Stop Solutions

Years ago, Lee Cockerell, the executive vice president of Walt Disney World, received a phone call routed through his office assistant. The caller had apparently been transferred numerous times to many people at Disney to attend to his request, but to that point, the situation was not resolved.

The executive quickly understood why the caller was confused. The accent on the other end of the phone was that of a German man who was trying to get help "fixing the monorail." The man was trying to get the right part; he had contacted more than 20 people around the property to get the part but had been unable to get it.

The situation was initially perplexing. Why was a monorail broken, and why were they calling him and every one else for a part he needed? After listening for some time, it became apparent what the problem was: This man had purchased a *toy* monorail for his grandson, and had returned to Germany to give it to him, only to discover that the monorail wasn't working. The man had made almost 20 calls and still couldn't get the part he needed to fix it. Cockerell immediately sent a replacement toy monorail to resolve that particular problem, but another problem remained: Why had this individual's call been passed on to so many others without being resolved? This created an opportunity to dramatically improve the nature of internal communication at Walt Disney World.

A key process is providing one-stop solutions. How many times have you experienced the following?

- Waiting for different people to get back to you with the information you needed.
- Having to dial through an "endless" phone tree searching for answers, perhaps only to end up leaving a message with no certainty of a reply.
- Being shuffled from one department to another, having to repeat the same information over and over.
- Being told "We don't handle that" or "That's not my job."

One way to provide customers with the gift of time is by providing one-stop solutions. This requires looking at processes in place to identify how they may be streamlined or improved.

The Buck Stops Here

Make it your company's mantra that employees take ownership of whatever problems they encounter. Unless the situation requires specific expertise that the employee doesn't have, he or she should feel empowered to settle the issue to the customer's satisfaction without hesitation.

For example, returning a shirt can become a huge hassle if the process isn't considered from the customer's point of view. Imagine you return to a store to exchange a shirt you purchased earlier. The sales associate informs you that he or she can't help you, that you'll need to go to customer service to process the exchange. Once you get to customer service, the associate informs you that he or she can't help you, and that you need to see the supervisor. After waiting for the supervisor to arrive, the supervisor tells you that before he or she can process the exchange, you'll need to fill out a form. By the time you go through all that extra effort, you might be justifiably upset.

If the employee is empowered to handle the situation immediately and satisfy the original reason you came to the store, the process allows for an opportunity to prevent further "cost" on behalf of the customer— hopefully, even adding value in some way. Even in cases where multiple functions need to be involved, processes can be established to allow frontline employees to work together to make the experience easier for the customer. Accountability can still be part of the process, it simply can be handled among the team or behind-the-scenes—away from the customer experience.

In sum, identify processes for which employees should take responsibility that enable them to work together effectively, retain accountability, and optimize the customer experience in the process.

Walk in Their Shoes

Again, "walking in the shoes" of your customers is critical (see chapter 2). Get on the phone and experience being placed on hold. Go online and find out how long it takes for your request to be returned. This is a good opportunity to see where streamlining some of your services may be of most value to your customer—and in your best interest. One city manager client we know calls departments after hours to learn, first hand, how efficient the process is.

Communicate Guidance

One of the outcomes of the monorail story mentioned above is that future monorail packages were relabeled with clear signage as to where to call in the event that there is a problem. This is now evident in many "ready-to-assemble" products. It's better for customers to make a call when they are confused than return the product to the store for a refund.

Provide an Employee Concierge

We typically think of a concierge as a great example of a person to whom customers can go when they need a one-stop solution. Not all employees can retain all the answers, so provide employees with access to a concierge type of resource when they need answers for the customers they are serving. Let the subject matter experts be accessible by all employees, rather than just a select few.

Provide Employee Tools

Give employees resources that help them quickly access the solutions they need. This is where recent technology advancements pay off to connect to already existing IT networks.

Connect the Customer Directly to the Customer

The same IT solutions that provide employees answers can often be routed directly to the customers themselves. Numerous companies with an online presence have identified the most-identified problems or most-asked questions and then, while working to solve those concerns, provide easy access to interim solutions. This solution not only helps them to save time but also saves you labor and other resources.

Providing Continuous Improvement

In the pursuit of highly satisfied customers, you need to identify a system for tracking and monitoring progress in providing high-quality service to customers on an ongoing basis. Because the frontline employees are closest to the customer, involving them in creating solutions that are the "right fit" is profoundly valuable. Though higher-level formal systems like Six Sigma or Kaizan may be valuable for specific types of organizations that require meticulous measurement processes, all organizations can generate significant results from involving employees in a less technical effort to make continuous improvements (see case study that follows).

Case Study: Starbucks Coffee Company

Starbucks Coffee Company has been working to improve its operations by focusing on the time it takes baristas to create the concoctions it sells. One fun way to help Starbucks team members generate solutions is with Mr. Potato Head toys. Regional trainers challenge teams to assemble the toy in timed activities followed by discussions about applying insights to their store operations. Starbucks has determined that 30 percent of a barista's time is spent in activities such as walking, reaching, and bending. When they put the beans in a different location, or make it more convenient to access ingredients, they save time that can then be reinvested into value-added activities for the customer.

The trick is not discovering ways to save time; it is identifying the best place to spend the time you save. One answer might be in hiring fewer employees and cutting labor since it no longer takes as many people to do the job when you integrate those improvements—passing the savings on to your customers. Another response might be to reduce the amount of time customers have to wait to get served. An equally appropriate response might be to repurpose that saved time to doing other jobs that need more attention, such as keeping the facility clean.

For Starbucks, however, it's about the social experience. The Starbucks brand leads the employees—or "partners" as the company calls them—to focus on maximizing interaction time with their customers. The bottom line: It's the application of these delivery Ps in alignment with your values and your promise that sets you apart in the minds of your customers. (Jargon 2009)

There are many customized continuous improvement processes. They essentially consist of these steps:

1. Measure.
2. Act.
3. Re-Measure.
4. Evaluate.

These first four steps are more common. The fifth step is the most missed, and critical to successful continuous improvement, so many world-class organizations have added it:

5. Celebrate/Share.

Here are the steps in more detail.

Measure

To track and measure customer comments, employees must be attentive. In essence, everyone can be a "listening post" or source of information gathering. There are numerous ways to listen to customers. Information may include formal research that was previously documented, letters and emails, and financial records. All these vehicles are measurement efforts.

Here's one example of how to use opportunities available to you to respond operationally to what customers want. While conducting your daily business, you may occasionally hear people ask about an item you don't currently carry. You've heard it mentioned once or twice, so you think to ask in your weekly meeting if others have been asked for that particular product. Others have as well, so the team decides to keep track of the number of times customers ask for that particular product. Keeping track may be as simple as keeping a sheet of paper behind the counter with tick marks on it, helping you monitor customer interest. You may even ask (without leading the customers) at the point of purchase if there is anything else they wanted but couldn't find. The end result is that within a reasonable timeframe, you can discover whether this is indeed a product worth pursuing for the benefit of your customer—and your revenues. So this is step one—measuring customer interests, requests, complaints, and ideas.

Suppose that, after analyzing your situation over some period, you determine that there was indeed genuine interest in the new idea. What's next?

Act

Joseph Gardner (2009), director of talent acquisition and development at the Gaylord National Hotel, captures the mission of a leader during a change initiative well. He states that the leader's role is threefold: (1) about 5 percent of the leader's job is to build relationships and alliances; (2) about 5 percent of the leader's job is to build awareness about operational challenges and issues and gather knowledge; and (3) 90 percent of the leader's job is to develop action. A great leader, anywhere in the organization, is known for a bias for action.

For many, this is the step that is the most difficult. Resistance to committed action takes many forms, but often is simply continuing to analyze (and overanalyze), embracing the excuse to avoid risking failure. This has been jokingly referred to as "analysis paralysis." Unfortunately, in the business world, taking no action can be the riskiest thing a person can do.

To push past any resistance to initiating possible solutions to the situation, it is best to adopt a bias for responsible action. Some call this "Ready! Fire! Aim!"—indicating a willingness to experiment with new possibilities and learn during the process. Disney had another way of saying it: "80 and Go!" This refers to the strategy that in most cases (other than safety or ethical issues), better results came from getting about 80 percent confident that you were on the right solution and then taking action. When intense focus and effort were invested into this process, the final solutions came faster, more cheaply, and more effectively. So, to develop this kind of a bias for action:

1. *Keep it small:* Test the idea at a smaller scale. If the idea works, then move to a larger scale, but don't invest too many resources until you've tested it.

2. *Act quickly:* Don't wait until you've generated dozens of further reports and collected endless data. Get out of the gate and just do it! Then readjust as you get further insight (which is covered in the evaluate step).

The key thing is to do something as soon as you see a trend or pattern that looks promising. Remember, the point to this process is to learn and grow. Unless you try new approaches, you will never get better solutions. The way you know whether or not your new idea is better is to measure again and compare with the initial measurement.

Re-Measure

Once you have acted on something, it's time to re-measure to see if the solution that was put in place fulfilled the opportunity in question. Remember to use a similar process of measurement so you can be confident your results show a legitimate result—one way or another.

Evaluate

To evaluate, you simply compare the intended learning outcome with the results achieved by the experiment. The important thing here is to approach the information in an unbiased way. The goal of participating in this improvement process is to learn something valuable that can add value to your customers or your team. If the new idea worked on a small scale, then move on to implementing it on a larger scale, as necessary. If it didn't work, then learn from this and identify another solution to best use the opportunity.

Remember that this is a cyclical process. You measure, take action, re-measure, evaluate, and repeat as necessary.

Celebrate/Share

This step is the most missed in customer service measurement. After going through the four-step cycle described above, it's important to recognize everyone's efforts in conducting the process; even if the desired results were not achieved, everyone should have learned something of value. The important thing is that you actively focused on improving the customer experience, and the efforts of all should be valued and recognized.

Your way of celebrating can vary. It doesn't have to be big, but it should be appropriate to the effort made, and it should be personalized. Ask the team how they want to celebrate, and make the experience fun. Doing so creates an environment where others are more willing to learn from their experience in improving what they do and how they do it next time.

It's equally important that you share your results with others. Sharing with others breaks down silos and helps others. Sharing allows other colleagues to benchmark and learn from you. Moreover, sharing keeps others from making the mistakes you've already made.

You can share your lessons in a number of ways—from submissions to the company newsletter to hosting an annual best practices symposium, where people involved with every function come together to share what they have learned. This creates internal opportunities for the organization, and it invites teams to present what they've learned in a creative way to others in the context of an open showcase.

Summing Up

When you truly lead with your customer, you gain a partner in making everything you do better. Processes are what connects all aspects of the customer experience. When done well, not only will you improve every step of your Six P Customer Formula, but you'll also strengthen your relationship with your customer—creating better sales, advocacy, and results.

Next steps for building the brand through process:

✦ How can you make waiting more valuable for customers?

✦ How can you deliver service more consistently?

✦ How can you give the gift of time to customers?

✦ Technology is often employed to create efficiencies. How can you use technology to improve your customers' experience?

✦ What options might you give customers to optimize their service experience?

✦ How can you streamline solutions so customers get the answers and help they want the first time?

✦ Have you challenged your team to own the customer problems they encounter?

✦ How can you continually measure and improve upon the service you provide?

Chapter 15

Delivering Products and Services They Really Want

Many business professionals tend to consider that delivering value to customers merely involves issues of products and services—P5, in the context of the World Class Excellence Model (see figure 4-1). World-class companies make the extra effort to clearly distinguish products from people, place, and processes. Though it's not easy to place any multifaceted experience in simple, separate buckets, thinking critically can open up opportunities that can give you a competitive edge.

Leading businesses see *all* the variables in what they offer. Although the focal point of any purchase is the ultimate product or service, you must also pay attention to many other variables if you wish to stand out among your peers.

Focusing on products and services while clarifying other aspects of the service delivery tool is challenging, especially when there can be a gradation of the products and services themselves. For instance, a hospital's primary role is to improve the patient's health. Prescribing medications is one part of that responsibility, but the medication as a product is actually separate from the service of prescribing the medication. In other words, you can prescribe the right medication, but if the in-hospital pharmacy fails to fill the prescription correctly or deliver it properly, then the experience can be severely compromised.

Or take the example of renting a hotel room. Though most might view the room as "the" product, other things also support that hotel room experience—towels, shampoos, bedding, clock radios, ironing boards, and so forth. None of these lesser items is the primary product or service being rented, but because they all contribute to the guest's experience, it is best to also consider them as products. World-class companies consider secondary products to be part of the product package.

Westin offers a great example of how a world-class organization pays attention to such matters. After a thorough overhaul of its approach to branding, it committed to improving the entire sensory experience of its guests. It began an ongoing campaign that includes secondary products, such as scented candles in the lobby. These brand-expanding new products have become product lines of their own—the Heavenly Bed, the Heavenly Bath, and even the Heavenly Dog Bed. Note that these products are not limited to the original product—the room itself. It's the attention to these related details that helps differentiate them in the marketplace. In fact, this effort made such a difference in the industry that Westin's competitor Marriott, traditionally the leader in hotel innovation, followed suit with its own Marriott Bed and other retail products.

Creating Tangible Memories

Ultimately, your brand will be associated with whatever products you deliver. Think about the bigger picture: How can you better leverage your product to create additional benefits for your organization? The goal is to connect your tangible item as a reminder of the superior value of that experience—so whenever your customers see that item afterward, they reexperience the positive memories and want to return or refer your business to others. Of course, there are several facets to consider when creating your own tangible memory:

+ Providing competitively superior products and services.
+ Impressing through design, display, and packaging.
+ Balancing quality and quantity.
+ Balancing choices and streamlining.

+ Providing product support.
+ Continually improving your product.

Providing Competitively Superior Products and Services

You've probably met individuals who have brand loyalty—to a particular product, for example, Chevy versus Ford. Enthusiasts may be able to differentiate by the car's body shape, but the vast majority of car components—think brands of air bags or fuel injection systems—are much less obvious to the typical buyer. Are these kinds of details a true differentiator that can cause one organization to stand out over another?

Differentiation is one way you can add value—and influence customers to pay more for your product. Though customers will not ignore price, many factors influence a customer's choice. How do we create additional value and a competitive edge? By deeply listening to customers and understanding them via the Customer Compass, and by taking action to align and/or improve the product based on that definition. World-class businesses understand that, ultimately, the customer defines what is different and better, and what really matters.

Impressing Through Design, Display, and Packaging

Great organizations often find creative ways to design, package, and display their product. They follow proven design principles to package in a way that gets—and keeps—the attention of the potential customer. Some organizations are even finding ways to be more environmentally savvy in their packaging to appeal to the growing trend of the general public's environmental interests.

Imagine that your product was so beautiful that people treated it as a piece of art. The genius behind the sensual look and feel of products made by Apple is Jonathan Ive, its vice president of industrial design. Apple products are such beautiful sculptural pieces that they are featured in the permanent collections of museums worldwide, including the Museum of Modern Art in New York and the Centre Pompidou in Paris.

According to Ive, it's really about making a product accessible, not intimidating. As he sees it, the consumer is surrounded by multitudes of products made by companies that really don't care about their design. When these companies don't care enough to focus on these details, their customers can be easily lured away.

The same is true for the presentation of the product. If your product is unique, shouldn't you also display it in a unique way? Notice how differently organizations like Wal-Mart and Apple display their products in their stores. The desired brand experience of each company has a strong influence on that decision. Regardless of packaging details, one common truth is that cluttered packaging and displays can reduce the product's desirability. When a product isn't readily accessible, the investment of time and effort on behalf of the customer increases—undermining the value of the experience.

The virtual world (the Internet, telephone, and so on) has its own set of challenges regarding presentation. As with the physical world, the best product can be poorly showcased online. The same foundational issues exist regardless of which arena your business is in; you must follow strong design principles to package in a way that draws strong attention to the product.

And then there is packaging. Recently, "frustration-free packaging" has been a goal of organizations like Johnson & Johnson, Microsoft, Fisher-Price, and Nike. Target committed to reducing the polyvinyl chloride plastics used in many of its products and packaging. This is an effort to address environmental and toxicity concerns as well as to curtail clamshell-packaging injuries. The Consumer Product Safety Commission noted that each year almost 7,000 individuals require emergency room care in what's been referred to by Amazon's CEO as "wrap rage." Numbers in the United Kingdom suggested that more than 70,000 have been to a hospital, all due to the "effects of packaging." This includes anything from children suffocating in plastic bags to injuries of people using scissors to open cartons. Obviously, customers are leading product providers to make significant packaging changes that ultimately affect the customer experience. Ensuring the packaging adds value—or doesn't decrease value—should be an important priority.

Balancing Quality and Quantity

The word "quality" suggests superiority of some kind—a degree or grade of excellence. "Quantity" generally means "a specified number or amount." Generally held principles of economics indicate a correlation between supply and demand. When uncontrolled, an increase in quantity can often result in a lack of quality. The general public often assumes that fast food restaurants selling convenience meals at a low price will have products that are poorer in taste—and possibly even unhealthy. On the other hand, the lack of availability of a particular model of sports car compared with other (more available) brands can lead to the impression that the less available product is in higher demand and, therefore, of much better quality.

Is it possible to successfully balance quality and quantity to optimize brand value? Wal-Mart, which has consistently been at or toward the top of the *Fortune* 100 firms for decades, is perhaps the best example of quality balanced with quantity and the importance of public perception. Wal-Mart's emphasis is on offering quantity discounts over high-quality products. Several other companies are extremely successful regarding product quality/quantity concerns as well, considering that popular lifestyles and a sense of happiness revolve around the products sold and marketed by these companies.

Another place successfully balancing the quality-versus-quantity challenge is TGI Friday's, which announced an initiative called "Right Portion at the Right Price." In response to health care professionals, who protest the large meal portions Americans are receiving, TGI Friday's now offers smaller portions at a reduced price. Though this shift has reduced the overall meal ticket, it has also increased traffic into the restaurant to the point of adding to overall revenue compared with the previous year. Other industry competitors—like Subway, Quizno's, Pizza Hut, and Boston Market—have followed with similar programs.

Balancing Choices and Streamlining

One common business belief is that customers want options. The general thinking is that the more choices a customer has, the more the customers will find something they want and will purchase it. Contrary to the common mindset, the most successful businesses have discovered that too many choices can actually make it difficult for customers to sort through it all—adding confusion and ultimately undermining sales.

A classic example of this is Apple's reemergence in 1997. The Apple product line had become cluttered with a range of choices that were not effectively responding to its customers' needs. When founder Steve Jobs returned to the company, one of the first things he did was streamline the product line. Even the logo went from a band of rainbows to a solid image. Everything was simplified.

Many online companies have succeeded because they are able to provide a range of choices that a standard "big box" store could not keep in stock. Identify what works best for the products you offer and create a balance between choices and a streamlining of the experience.

Providing Product Support

Think about how your customer will begin using your product—are there instructions? Have you put one of these products together yourself? This is where walking in the shoes of your customer is critical. It's amazing how a simple thing like poor instructions can create a frustrating customer experience—even when the product is otherwise very strong.

There are many ways to provide product support—from the purchaser to the manufacturer. Organizations offer toll-free numbers to call centers that answer questions from customers all over the world. Perhaps the most famous one is the Butterball Turkey line started in 1981, which offers last-minute directions to novice household chefs everywhere. This product-support initiative, which has extended to websites and blogs, generates tremendous goodwill and public relations for the organization every holiday season. This is in marked contrast to other toll-free numbers that lead to long phone trees and difficult-to-understand service representatives.

In recent years, online support has become the king of product support. Many organizations have made it into a small profit-making arm, charging for support, or getting customers to buy an additional product support package at the time of their purchase. Other companies offer complimentary product support as a way to differentiate their product from others. The critical thing is to provide not only product support but also customer-centered support that really adds value to your product offering.

Continually Improving Your Product

Great organizations are always engaged in the quest to improve their products. Technology in particular has become too much a part of overall corporate success for its effectiveness to be left to chance. That said, no matter how complex your product is, managing quality is mandatory for retaining customer loyalty. In the last decade, process improvement initiatives have become more prevalent. Here are some of the more familiar of these programs:

+ *SPC—Statistical Process Control,* pioneered by Walter A. Shewhart in the 1920s and applied by W. Edwards Deming during World War II. Its success is based on monitoring processes through data control charts.
+ *TOC—Theory of Constraints,* developed by Eliyahu M. Goldratt, which operates on the premise that every organization has at any given point at least one constraint limiting the system's performance relative to its goal. Organizations like Lucent, Lockheed Martin, and Boeing have successfully implemented TOC principles.
+ *The ISO 9001:2000,* which is maintained by the International Organization for Standardization, is primarily a family of standards for quality management systems.
+ *Lean Manufacturing/TPS* was mastered by the Japanese and then promoted by Toyota (which calls it the Toyota Production System). This approach focuses on creating more value with less work. Curiously, when Toyota benchmarked the production process in the United States, its staff found the best solution not in other automotive companies but during a visit to a Piggly Wiggly

supermarket, where they saw how the stores only reordered and restocked goods once the customers had bought them.

◆ *Six Sigma,* a methodology for improvement shaped by companies such as Motorola, Honeywell, and General Electric, seeks to identify and remove the causes of defects and errors in both manufacturing and business processes. Its name comes from the notion that if one has six standard deviations between the mean of a process and the nearest specification limit, practically no items will fail to meet the specifications. Most *Fortune* 500 companies have begun Six Sigma initiatives with the aim of reducing costs and improving quality.

These recognized and proven quality-control programs are rising in popularity as more technology managers are looking for ways to help remove degrees of risk and uncertainty from their business equations, and to introduce methods of predictability that better ensure success. These are no longer mere company- or employee-driven initiatives. Customers are now invited, via the Internet, to be part of their product improvement programs. Enter the serial number for your John Deere product and you'll have access to benefits from ongoing product improvement programs. Adobe, which hosts the Adobe Product Improvement Plan, feels that this plan is a great way for customers to provide them with feedback in the same way as user groups, focus groups, and participation in prerelease programs.

The bottom line: No matter what your product, you must continually improve it for your customers. And remember, your customers determine what is and is not important.

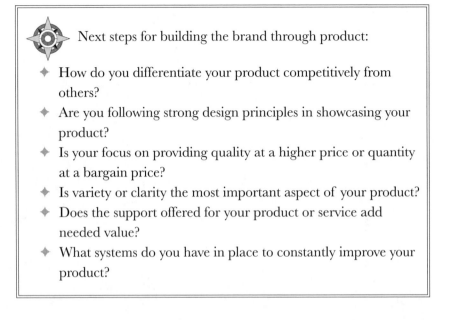

Next steps for building the brand through product:

✦ How do you differentiate your product competitively from others?

✦ Are you following strong design principles in showcasing your product?

✦ Is your focus on providing quality at a higher price or quantity at a bargain price?

✦ Is variety or clarity the most important aspect of your product?

✦ Does the support offered for your product or service add needed value?

✦ What systems do you have in place to constantly improve your product?

Chapter 16

Creating Loyalty and Profits with the Right Price

After outlining the promise and exploring how world-class companies deliver on the promise via people, place, process, and product, it's time to turn to what confirms the value of the customer experience: the price—P6, in the context of the World Class Excellence Model (see figure 4-1).

The term "price" specifically refers to the true cost and value to the customer. Value is what the customer gains from the experience of purchasing your product or service—a combination of a superior product provided by superior people, who create a place that is engaging and deliver a seamless process. Remember, world-class organizations follow the Six Ps Customer Formula:

Promise < People + Place + Process + Product > Price

You've heard the expression, "Well worth the price"? That's what this formula means—that the price is less than or at least equal to the entire experience, which includes the product as well as the people, place, and process. Keep in mind that, to create or maintain a competitive edge, "equal" isn't acceptable; the value must exceed the price paid.

On the basis of their ability, people are willing to pay the price, depending on how they value the quality of the people, place, process, and product. Or vice versa, the poorer the people, place, process, and product the less customers are willing to pay.

To address a common misunderstanding, let's explore what customers really pay for the services they receive. The true cost isn't measured in just dollars and cents; it's broken down into two categories: tangible and intangible.

The Tangible Price Customers Pay

The tangible price is a more quantifiable cost. It's reflected in money, time, effort, and resources. Let's briefly consider each one.

Money

The most obvious tangible cost to the customer is in the amount of currency he or she pays to receive the goods and services you are delivering. There are other costs to the customer that are tangible. Clearly this is an important arena to consider, but it isn't the only one.

Time

They say time is money. How long does it take to get to the hospital? How long does it take to wait for treatment or help in the emergency room? Processing these waits, and having beds available along with needed staff, are major investments, but they are part of the price patients must pay if their lives are at stake.

The same could be said for shopping online. How long does it take to make that online purchase? How long must the customer wait for the product to be delivered? All these are tangible to the customer in terms of their personal time. Zappos explains that it takes up to four days to receive a pair of shoes purchased online. But their location, next to FedEx in Memphis, means that the shoes often show up the next day. People appreciate the value from the time saved waiting for their shoes.

Effort

How much of an effort do customers have to expend to make the purchase? Did they have to give up their lunch hour to make it? Did they lose a night's sleep to get that bargain sale item the day after Thanksgiving? That notable retail day, known as Black Friday, is a favorite for those ready for a great deal. Wal-Mart has negated the hassle of needing to go from store to store to find the best deal by matching any Black Friday ad. In fact, rather than being forced to wait until the actual sale day, more and more stores are offering their sales earlier and for longer periods of time to lure customers to buy. Moreover, others like Amazon, Target, and Best Buy offer big discounts a few days later on Cyber Monday, when it will be even easier for shoppers to make their purchases. Even online retailers are extending their sales strategies to better exceed the expectations of the customer's sense of price.

Resources

Other resources required to complete the experience of the purchase include a wide variety of possible "investments," such as

+ the favor your customer asked of friends to drive them to your store
+ an unfortunate incident that occurs on the way to the store
+ the additional components they had to purchase to utilize your product or service.

The Intangible Price Customers Pay

"Intangible" simply means the things that can't be measured. Examples of intangible costs include missed purchases, how it makes you feel, how it helps others, and how it appears to others. Again, let's briefly consider each one.

Missed Purchases

What opportunities did the customer miss out on to purchase the product or service? The sacrifice made when deciding to go on vacation may be postponing a mortgage payment, or eating peanut butter and jelly sandwiches the remainder of the year to afford the trip. Because money is limited for most people, customers pay a price for not being able to purchase other things.

How It Makes You Feel

Returning to the essential customer needs: Does it require your customers to lose control? Does it require them to sacrifice stability? Does it result in them feeling less significant? These are serious costs that affect the decision as to whether your customers pay the price. Related feelings can be positive or negative. Many motorcycle enthusiasts are willing to pay a higher price to ride a "hog"—that's why they shop at Harley-Davidson—it's about the status, the way they feel as they hear the distinctive growl of the motor and see the Harley logo on the side of the gas tank.

How It Helps Others

Customers are often willing to pay the price for the sake of others. In its simplest form, you find this on birthdays or holidays when someone purchases a gift for a loved one. They are willing to pay a price to be connected with others. In charitable terms, many people today are willing to pay a price that might return help to others less fortunate. In environmental terms, people also pay a premium price for goods and services that help the environment.

How It Appears to Others

The reason many pay the price is for status and acceptance. Many pay a premium price to look stylish, hip, or cool. There is also a "price" paid for not looking stylish, hip, or cool.

Whatever the price—tangible and intangible—it must be equal to or less than what was promised—the first P of the World Class Excellence Model (see figure 4-1). The price must be equal to or less than what they received from the people, product, place, and process. Customers are willing to invest themselves as necessary, if the complete experience creates sufficient value for them. Consider, for example, the following case study from Ikea.

An Example: Ikea

Ikea demonstrates how the price should be equal to, better than, or less than the value of the people, place, process, and product. Ikea did not approach its business by seeking to create the best products possible at the highest price point possible. Rather, it sought to offer a wide range of well-designed but functional home furnishing products at prices so low that most people could afford them.

The name "Ikea" comes from the initials of Ingvar Kamprad, a Swedish man who grew up in Elmtaryd and Agunnaryd, the farm and village whose names provide the last two initials in "Ikea." There, the soil was thin and poor—and people had to live frugally and with very limited resources. Starting a business by selling matches, Kamprad scraped together whatever he could to create opportunities for his customers. From these humble values, he built a multimillion-dollar home furnishings brand with nearly 250 stores in more than 30 countries.

On the wall near the exit of the Ikea stores is a set of statements designed to address Ikea's price proposition. It begins with the promise: Ikea provides good quality and design at a low price. Here is how it aims to deliver this promise:

Why ... are Ikea prices so low with such good quality and design? Why do our designers create the price tag first?

By starting at a low price goal, Ikea designers find clever ways to create high-quality furniture you can afford. That's why.

Why do we make so many of everything?

By producing and distributing in bulk, we get huge discounts, which you enjoy, in lower prices. That's why.

Why are we so obsessed with keeping things flat?

Ikea furniture is flat-packed, so it's cheaper for us to ship and store. You see the savings in lower prices. That's why.

Why do we abuse our home furnishings?

Ikea furniture endures rigorous tests, so you can be sure before you buy that it can take just about anything. That's why.

Why isn't there more staff to answer questions?

The answers are on the price tag! By helping yourself, you reduce the need for staff and keep prices lower. That's why.

Why should I deliver my own furniture?

Taking it home yourself lets you enjoy it today! (Remember, when stores say "free delivery," that means it's already been added to your furniture price.) That's why.

Why would I want to assemble the furniture myself?

To save money! Doing it yourself (even if it can be tricky) saves you the high costs of factory assembly. That's why.

In the context of the Six Ps Customer Formula, the Ikea case study translates into table 16-1.

Beyond what Ikea will share, there are also other "costs" involved. One is that of the quality of their furniture. At first glance, it looks like there are a lot of mix-and-match choices to make, but on closer inspection, it's actually a fairly homogenous Scandinavian-style choice. Ikea notably succeeds in difficult economies, when people are looking for solid choices at the lowest price. Though Ikea was ranked 16th among furniture-only retailers a few years ago, it is now number two. These are impressive, world-class results—in any economy.

Table 16-1. Ikea's Six Ps in the Context of the Loyalty Formula

P	Description
Promise	Good quality and design for a low price
Less than ...	
People	Smaller staff
Place	Large warehouses to house wide selection and quantity
Process	Large quantity You deliver your own furniture You assemble your own furniture
Product	Furniture undergoes rigorous testing Furniture is flat-packed
All of which is greater than ...	
Price	A low price

The best-in-business organization always studies the tangible and intangible costs to any customer, and it factors those in as it seeks to deliver the best products and services possible. It's truly about the Six Ps Customer Formula:

Promise < People + Place + Process + Product > Price

Next steps for building the brand through price:

+ What tangible price do your customers pay in terms of money, time, effort, and resources?
+ How can we lower the price other than by lowering the sticker price?
+ What intangible price does your customer pay?
+ What price is your customer willing to pay for intangible benefits? How can you reduce the intangible price?

Part IV

Ensuring Alignment and Integrity

Chapter 17

How Service "Netting" Gets Results

In this and the other three chapters of part IV, we explore the implementation aspect of transforming your culture and brand. The key aspects here are ensuring that your behaviors are aligned with your core vision and values and have integrity. Integrating world-class excellence requires using all the components of the models we've introduced to anticipate the customer experience, recover well when the unexpected happens, lead your employees through a transformation initiative, and sustain continuous improvement to build a lasting legacy of excellence.

Most organizations often talk about service recovery. Service recovery is important, but rarely done well. Part of the problem is that the recovery process occurs after the initial damage has been done. World-class organizations have found a better way to ensure a superior customer experience, which we call "service netting." To explain the concept of service netting, it's useful to use the metaphor of a high-wire act in a circus. You wouldn't hesitate to place a safety net underneath a trapeze act in case a performer falls. This is the same foundational thinking behind service netting, which means establishing preventive steps to keep poor service from happening in the first place. In stark contrast, focusing only on service recovery is the equivalent of not providing a net but, instead, having a very efficient plan to call the ambulance after an accident.

Although service recovery is a reactive measure, providing service netting is a proactive effort. World-class organizations don't wait for bad things to happen to their customers—they do what they can to anticipate and prevent them. Service netting requires walking in the shoes of the customers in advance to understand the experience, and then putting "just in case" systems in place to ensure the best for the customer—even if a mistake happens. According to Pam Eyring (2009), of the Protocol School of Washington, "The key to any successful event or service experience is to anticipate the needs of your guests at any given time. Once you really understand your guest's perspective, you can design their experience—step by step—with the goal of exceeding their expectations at every turn. When you get the details right, you can actually make memories that last a lifetime."

One approach to creating a service net is to look at the current service and identify those moments that most often disappoint your customers. When are they most often complaining? What do you need to apologize about most often? When do you have to give money back, or replace an item? These incidents are costly in many ways: money, time, employee morale, and—most important—the cost to the customer's experience, their relationship with your company, and your company's resulting reputation.

Track these circumstances that make you vulnerable and identify how you can "catch" customers before they have a poor experience. Remember, the strongest, most effective nets are composed of many strands woven tightly together. You may need to put more than one solution in place to catch customers before they "hit the ground" and become upset. World-class organizations involve all employees in identifying and providing those solutions.

Netting through the Six Ps

We've spent several chapters delving into the best-in-business practices found in applying the six Ps. Before continuing, it is useful to summarize the key points for the six Ps; see table 17-1. World-class organizations

Table 17-1. The Key Points of the Six Ps

P	Internal Customers—Culture	External Customers—Brand
Promise: Take integrity personally	The organizational culture	The brand promise
People: Everyone engages his or her customer	Those serving those on the front line	Those serving the front line
Place: Consider the customer domain	The "backstage" setting for your employees	The "onstage" setting for your services and offerings
Process: Make it easy to do business with you	Employee guidelines, rules, and policies	The policies, procedures, and rules that govern the delivery of your products and services
Product: Provide the best of what they really want	The employee offerings you provide	The goods and services you offer to external customers
Price: True costs determine value	Tangible and intangible costs to the employee	Tangible and intangible costs to the external customer
Summary: The Six Ps Customer Formula	Promise < People + Place + Process + Product > Price	

don't just talk about excellence; they accomplish it by design. They successfully bring dreams, words, and goals to life. As they integrate the insights and methods related to the six Ps and pursue them to create a high-performing culture and a compelling brand, it's as if they're constructing a strong service net that's able to hold up both internal and external customers. Now let's begin connecting the strands that make up this net and then consider several tools that you can use to implement your own transformation to achieve world-class excellence.

Integrating Your Values

Many baby boomers recall Farrell's Ice Cream Parlour, a favorite local hangout that saw its heyday during the 1960s and 1970s. It was a popular destination restaurant for many. And it succeeded on one core value—

Fabulous Fun! The people, the place, the process, and the product were entirely fun. Here are some examples of why it was so fun:

✦ *Place:* A turn-of-the-century atmosphere with an old-fashioned candy store up front, marble counters, red-flocked wallpaper, and dark wood paneling, all surrounded by hundreds of blinking lights and the sound of a player piano.

✦ *People:* Magical moments where enthusiastic employees dressed in straw boater hats and pinstriped vests would run around the restaurant delivering an $8^1/_2$-pound ice cream concoction known as "the Zoo" or would award those who ate an entire "Pig Trough" a special ribbon.

✦ *Process:* Employees came by your table to sing happy birthday, bestowing free ice cream to those who signed up.

✦ *Product:* Old-fashioned paper menus adorned with Gibson girls announced a fanciful food selection with names like Pike's Peak, Tin Roof, and the Gastronomical Delicatessen Epicurean Delight.

Farrell's was an experience loaded with fun. Even the employees weren't the typical "soda jerks." They were "builders of fountain fantasies."

So what happened? Farrell's went from being sold to Marriott, which expanded the experience, to being sold to a San Francisco investment group, which diminished the experience. By the 1980s, everything that had been fun about Farrell's had changed into a traditional family-style restaurant. The focus was no longer ice cream but food variety. The ambiance had been softened to attract business customers during lunch. And budget cutbacks, from the piano to the pickle on the side, had created a fairly bland, if not tired, experience. In short, "Fabulous Fun" had left the building. Even the birthday list was allegedly sold to the Selective Service. Eventually, mall food courts became the rage, and McDonald's took over the children's markets with its happy meals and playgrounds.

The message is that it isn't simply enough to run a good restaurant with good employees in a nice setting. Ultimately, it's about the degree in which you declare your values in your business. Farrell's was about Fabulous Fun. When the fun *experience* was removed, it became just another restaurant in a competitive climate. But when it was fun, it was unique, exciting, and—most important—profitable.

This is not a message about making your restaurant fun. It's about identifying your core vision and values, and infusing those values into all that you do—and all that your customer experiences.

You've heard about providing exceptional value to customers—but what does that mean, tactically? It means that your values are so operationally embedded throughout the entire six Ps that your experience becomes preferred by your customers—both external and internal.

The Integrity Net

According to the *Harvard Business Review* (1997), "Service is not only a matter of being pleasant to customers—just as being a doctor is not only a matter of having a comforting bedside manner—but also of understanding the systems that make customer satisfaction possible, ... understanding how and why the whole system works is the fundamental expertise of service professionals."

Although there is much that can be resolved by a pleasant disposition, a smile can't make up for shoddy policies and procedures, or for a product that is flawed and poorly designed. Customer service is more than a smiling face. It's about attending to all the details—what we refer to as "everything speaks." Everything sends a message through the service you deliver.

To help design a world-class experience, we've created the Integrity Net, a simple tool that has transformed many operations just like yours. This tool provides an "operational snapshot" that helps analyze your business in a comprehensive, yet simple (not simplistic) view of the details that make an impact on your customer service experience—whether external customers or internal customers (employees). The Integrity Net has two aspects:

1. Identifying those operational values that are at the core of your brand or culture.
2. Reflecting these operational values across all six Ps that fold into the experience.

Using the Integrity Net, table 17-2 gives an example of how effective service tactics can support a fitness club's operational values of safe and clean, cutting edge, and supportive to the fitness club member experience. You can construct your own net for your organization, using the blank table 17-3.

Key Points

Several important considerations shape the value of the Integrity Net:

◆ *External versus internal:* The fitness club example given in table 17-2 offers a glimpse of how service could be optimized for the external customer experience. Attending to these relevant details builds both a stronger culture and a more solid brand.

◆ *Strategic and tactical:* Using the Integrity Net documents, you create a service view for both management and the front line. Regardless of the role within your organization, the Integrity

Table 17-2. Sample Filled-In Integrity Net for a Fitness Club

	Safe and Clean	Cutting Edge	Supportive
Promise	You're here to attain stronger health, not to get injured or infected	You're not going to get this kind of experience elsewhere	You can't get this kind of support elsewhere
People	1:1 Training with all new members on proper use of equipment	Licensed/certified trainers; ongoing	Manager and staff on the floor and not behind the desk
Place	Drinking fountains are routinely cleaned and polished	Interactive kiosk acts as a juke box, allowing members to choose their favorite music	Wide array of TV channels to watch while working out
Process	Equipment is routinely checked and on a maintenance schedule	Interactive kiosk on the floor allows members to log their workout	Ladies Express Pass provided to key pieces of floor equipment
Product	Sanitized dry wipes available throughout to help prevent staph infections	Condition of the exercise equipment	A wide selection of equipment to choose from
Price	I don't want to be seen as the one person who doesn't wipe down the equipment	Worth the drive from my house to get the workout I can't get anywhere else	Worth getting to know the staff; may even justify paying for a 1:1 trainer

Table 17-3. Sample Blank Integrity Net

	Value A	Value B	Value C	Value D
Promise				
People				
Place				
Process				
Product				
Price				

Net can help you focus on strategic and tactical concerns—both targeting a consistent, optimized attention to excellence.

✦ *Freedom within a framework:* The Integrity Net becomes vital guidance regarding the importance of the company's values, while providing employees latitude to identify and execute how these values will be "brought to life" using the delivery tools.

✦ *Integrity is key:* Consistency across all functions leads to integrity—which everyone in the organization can feel great about supporting. When employees feel that they deliver an important product or service and make a difference every day by being a part of a company that "walks the talk," commitment and buy-in increase dramatically.

◆ *Start with the low-hanging fruit:* When faced with not knowing where to start, use the Integrity Net to identify "quick wins" to provide noticeably superior service immediately, while continuing to develop larger, more complicated projects for implementation when resources allow.

◆ *Focus on the low-cost/no-cost criteria:* Nearly all world-class organizations begin every problem-solving exercise with the challenge to solve it using low-cost or no-cost solutions. Only when there is a significantly higher return on investment (whether tangible or intangible) should you entertain additional expenses.

◆ *The application of the Six Ps Customer Formula:* P1 < (P2 + P3 + P4 + P5) > P6. What you deliver (P2 + P3 + P4 + P5) should be better than what you promise (P1). And what your customers' experience should be worth more than the price (P6). Doing so creates superior customer value, loyalty/advocacy, better margins, and a world-class legacy.

◆ *Keep it simple, but not simplistic:* The most significant key of the Integrity Net is that it provides an elegant solution for achieving a comprehensive, fully integrated operation—one that is simple enough to legitimately be implemented in the real-life, everyday operation. This tool can span the gap between "knowing" and "doing."

An example of a leap in customer service due to strategically mapping the customer experience is shared by Nicola Millard (2009), customer experience futurologist for BT (formerly British Telecom), whose call center was struggling with handling complaints. BT wanted to resolve issues earlier to prevent dissatisfied customers and save unnecessary operational expenses. Millard explains:

> Complaints are opportunities to learn from customers and resolve issues. We found complaints to be about 4 percent of the traffic into

the traffic centre and, on average, each complaint generates seven subsequent calls (a big operational challenge). By proactively calling customers who looked as if they were about to complain, BT succeeded in increasing the number of customers who said they would recommend BT by 40 percent. We also were able to increase the number of customers who reported themselves to be very or extremely satisfied. We also significantly reduced the number of high-level complaints which reached the upper echelons on BT senior management.

Steps in Building an Integrity Net

To build your own Integrity Net, do the following:

1. Decide on the purpose: the customer experience (brand) or the employee experience (culture).
2. Determine the scope: What aspect of the customer or employee experience do you want to build out?
3. Outline the values that should shape this experience.
4. Identify P1: What you are promising (from the customer/employee perspective) relative to your values as they pertain to the scope of your analysis?
5. Brainstorm aligned solutions that exceed expectations with respect to the people, product, place, and process.
6. Establish the appropriate price for the quality of your product/service experience based on the tangible and intangible costs that your customer or employee must pay and their other available options.
7. Implement the action items identified throughout your Integrity Net.

Service Mapping

In addition to using the Integrity Net to attend to a single aspect of an experience, you can string together a series of matrixes to reflect the entire customer experience. We consider this a form of "service mapping." By identifying each step, or "moment of truth," of the experience, you can attend to the details that matter most to your customers—and create a seamless, extraordinary experience in the process.

Let's look at two examples of how to build your brand as well as your culture. The first one involves building the customer brand. Suppose you operate a fitness club. A matrix could be created for every step of the external customer experience, as shown in figure 17-1.

Figure 17-1. A Matrix for a Fitness Club Showing Steps in the Customer Experience

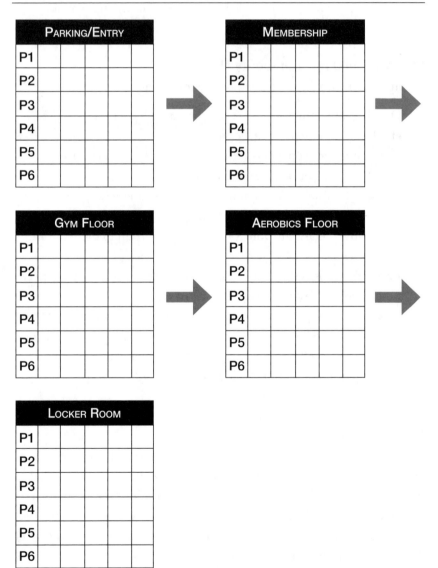

The second example shows how to build the employee culture. Replicating a series of matrixes for each step of the employees' "moments of truth" creates an opportunity to establish an extraordinary organizational culture—for example, the people management process, as shown in figure 17-2.

Figure 17-2. A Matrix for a People Management Process

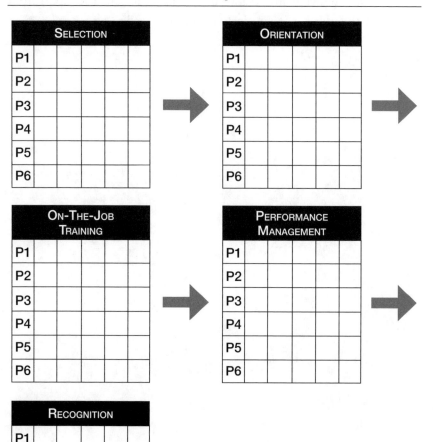

There are numerous other internal options that would create both improved integrity and effectiveness. You could map the budget cycle, the purchasing-approval process, the special events process—the options encompass any aspect of your business operation you want to improve. The goal is optimizing your internal customer's (employee's) experience as well. In summary, we offer a strong strategy for building a strong brand as well as a cohesive culture—for an organization that is set apart from the rest of the industry: achieving world-class excellence.

Chapter 18

Service Recovery That Really Works

Whatever the situation, you are best served when you apply the operational values defined and prioritized in part I of this book. A best-in-class organization does this for everyone who has an impact on its customers. That's Plan A. But what happens when your customer's experience doesn't go according to plan?

Unfortunately, no one will ever live in a perfect world. No matter how proactive you are, or how strong and integrated your service nets are, everyone occasionally makes mistakes. And then, the natural consequence of handling service recovery poorly would be other negative effects on your customers/compliers—and on your reputation, loyalty, and bottom line. In this respect, let's look at examples of relevant information from numerous research studies that have been common knowledge for years:

✦ Satisfied customers typically refer 5 new people to a product or service, while dissatisfied customers will complain to 10 people or more. Combine this dynamic with the belief that it can cost five to six times more to gain a new customer than keep an existing one, and there is plenty of justification for investing in a superior customer experience.

✦ Organizations, because of poor processes and/or uneducated or unmotivated employees, often make it difficult for customers to report a problem.

✦ Most customers won't complain—they simply do not return. Ironically, it's often your most passionate advocates who will complain, because they care about your business and want it to succeed.

✦ Despite common corporate assumptions, less than ½ percent of complaining customers are trying to "scam" the business (Stoller 2005). Most companies will institute strictly limited service recovery policies, claiming it is to "protect" losses from the ½ percent who abuse the system. The truth is that they do not save significant losses over those who do don't enforce such limiting policies—they simply irritate the 99½ percent of their honest customer base who need service recovery—making recovery even more unlikely.

✦ Service recovery processes, which require additional effort or time on behalf of the customer (filling out forms, waiting for a supervisor, and so on), usually negate whatever recovery effort is made on behalf of the company.

✦ One last commonly known saying you may have heard: "The customer is always right." What is not so commonly known is the opinion that world-class organizations hold about that saying: It is a lie. You've probably known for a long time that your customers are not always right. The perspective that world-class companies adopt allows for the truth and retains the all-important customer relationship: "The customer may not always be right, but they are always the customer. And if they are wrong, they will be wrong with dignity."

Identifying Appropriate Service Recovery Situations

What is the best approach to handle situations that failed to delight your customer? World-class service recovery must be appropriate for the (unique) situation, and enacted by the frontline employee who encounters the customer with the problem. There are two reasons for this:

1. When service recovery is more immediate, it results in higher customer satisfaction and greater loyalty.
2. Frontline staff, when trained properly, will be more effective and efficient in resolving customer situations than management—often spending less resources and getting better results.

The most successful organizations are prepared to respond to dissatisfied customers appropriately—even creating loyalty in the process! Remember, the primary element at the center of a service recovery situation is the relationship. All the issues that affect relationships (trust, communication, respect, concern, and the like) will come into play during this critical time. It is absolutely critical to treat any attempt to complain as an opportunity to strengthen your company's connection with this customer. World-class companies have found that, in some cases, they actually have a better relationship (with higher levels of customer satisfaction) after a service recovery interaction than if the interaction had never occurred!

Figure 18-1 shows a world-class model of service recovery that has been proven to help employees make the most effective decisions. This model was initially conceived by our colleagues Dennis Snow and Guy Smith, and it has found its way into organizations all over the world. This Service Recovery Matrix combines two criteria:

✦ *Severity:* How significant is the situation? How much has it affected the customer's experience with our organization? Consider the Customer Compass points introduced in part I.

✦ *Responsibility:* How responsible is your company for what has occurred? The key for assessing responsibility is to fix the situation with the specific customer first. It is only after the customer is satisfied that you should focus on accountability—who did what and how to resolve the root of the problem so it won't occur again.

To better explain the best option for repairing that customer's experience, on the basis of his or her unique circumstances, it is useful to consider an overview of the four quadrants of the service recovery model shown in figure 18-1.

Figure 18-1. Service Recovery Model

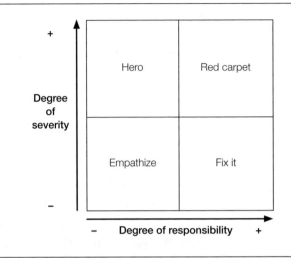

Low Severity/Low Responsibility

Starting at the lower left corner of figure 18-1, the first quadrant is low severity/low responsibility. When the situation is not very important to the customer, nor is it something for which your company is responsible, the best solution is to simply listen to the customer and *empathize* with him or her. When an issue is this inconsequential, the person usually just wants to be heard (one of the five essential customer needs). Saying "I'm sorry" isn't admitting fault—it is only communicating concern and care for the person who is somewhat unhappy.

Low Severity/High Responsibility

Moving to the lower right corner of figure 18-1, the second quadrant is low severity/high responsibility. When the situation isn't significant to the customer but the problem was caused by your company, the best thing to do is to *fix it* as quickly as possible, without calling attention to the situation. To "make a big deal" out of something when a customer considers it to be a minor issue only draws attention to the fact that there is a problem, which can actually encourage the customer to reconsider the perceived severity of the situation. When possible, it is a nice gesture to offer some small token of regret for the customer's inconvenience, such as a free cup of coffee or a lollipop for a child—depending on what is appropriate.

High Severity/High Responsibility

Moving to the upper right corner of figure 18-1, the third quadrant is high severity/high responsibility. Occasionally, big mistakes are made that are truly the fault of the company and that seriously undermine the customer's experience. When this happens, we are forced to *roll out the red carpet*—a big gesture is required to offset a big problem. In this situation, it is best to keep in mind that, in the mind of this customer, your company has broken its promise—and your attitude and actions should match that. Due to the severity of the problem, multiplied by the fact that your company is responsible, the customer will tend to be emotional, reactionary, and primed to spread the word. The immediate goal here is to do whatever possible to dissipate the emotion and begin to repair the trust that was lost by breaking your promise. The secondary goal is to follow up to make sure this never happens again.

High Severity/Low Responsibility

Finally, moving to the upper left corner of figure 18-1, the fourth quadrant is high severity/low responsibility. This is the quadrant that most companies get very, very wrong. Usually, when the responsibility is low, the typical response will be to match the lack of responsibility with an attempt to empathize. From the customer's perspective, this response is completely unacceptable. The impact on the customer experience is severe. They are vulnerable. They really *need* help to salvage the situation. What do world-class companies do instead? They see this as a great opportunity to *be a hero*.

Consider all the famous (or infamous) stories you've heard passionately shared about a service experience that makes or breaks a company's reputation—nearly all of them fall into this category. Nothing cements loyalty like a company that "saves the day" for a desperate customer—even when it wasn't the company's responsibility. Companies that respond to this customer's dire need with a smile and an "I'm sorry" are destined to be known by all who hear the story as "the company that didn't care."

World-class companies recognize these situations as valuable opportunities to make a difference—exceed expectations—and make a profound impression on that customer. You can't buy that kind of goodwill. And who wouldn't want to come to work every day if they know they had an opportunity to be a service hero?

Three Lessons about Service Recovery

There are three lessons to be learned about service recovery and for successfully implementing the lessons of the matrix shown in figure 18-1:

1. Empower the front line to respond immediately.
2. Generate low-cost/no-cost service ideas.
3. Net your recovery.

Let's look at each lesson.

Lesson 1: Empower the Front Line to Respond Immediately

Great organizations empower their frontline employees to deliver service recovery rather than limiting this responsibility only to management. There are several reasons why this works best:

+ The more immediate the recovery, the more the customer feels acknowledged. The longer they wait, or the more hoops they have to go through to resolve the issue, the more likely they will feel unappreciated as customers.
+ Immediate service recovery not only helps companies to retain their customers; it keeps the employees around as well. This is because they're empowered through training to make decisions that will satisfy their customers. Feeling like they have been heroes to customers can make them feel important and extremely satisfied.

In addition, well-trained frontline employees do a more effective job of offering service recovery than their managers. Supervisors often overcompensate because they have so many other responsibilities. Frontline employees typically are more connected with both the customer and the circumstances surrounding the issue.

One powerful example of effective service recovery training comes from the Ritz-Carlton hotel. Ritz-Carlton is known for fully empowering employees up to $2,000 a day for handling service recovery matters. This means that a housekeeper on duty could easily comp a few room nights without ever having to ask his or her manager. It also means that if employees request the assistance of a coworker, they can rely on their coworker to comply with the request. This doesn't happen by accident. Ritz-Carlton's leadership invests in this effort, and their operational effectiveness—and sterling reputation—is their return on this investment.

This approach is not about high-end hotels throwing money at problems. Each year, the moderately priced Hampton Inn chain refunds half of 1 percent of its total room revenue to dissatisfied guests. In the long run, this pays off for Hampton Inns. According to one industry expert, for every $1 refunded, the chain gets back an average of $7 in future business because the guest refers a new guest or returns—which probably would not have happened without the initial refund. Though this does not happen often, Hampton Inn staff members are provided with tools, such as those outlined in this book, to provide appropriate service recovery. In addition to these tools, coaching and daily lineups help involve associates in the process of optimizing the opportunities from these recovery scenarios (Stoller 2005).

World-class companies empower the front line simply to deliver on their promise—and realize world-class results.

Lesson 2: Generate Low-Cost/No-Cost Service Ideas

The most successful organizations make great profits and have the means to invest a lot of their budget into continuous improvement initiatives— and for the most part, they don't. Part of the mindset of extraordinary businesses is to make the most of their resources. This means two things to world-class companies:

1. Only spend what they need to. Using low-cost or no-cost solutions, whenever appropriate, frees up the remaining resources for other investments.
2. Leverage your best existing asset by involving frontline employees in generating and implementing creative problem-solving ideas.

According to many of these best-in-business organizations, some of their greatest breakthroughs have been the result of challenging the team to be innovative with existing (limited) resources, and exceed expectations regardless. Your staff members are already on your payroll. They know your business and your customers better than anyone else. Give them a real opportunity to show how resourceful they can get, and the results are sure to impress you—and your customers.

Lesson 3: Net Your Recovery

The goal of service recovery is not only to recover the quality of the customer's experience but also to recover a solution to that particular problem so that it never happens again. When you offer service recovery for the same problem over and over, that's a clear indication that you need to create better service nets.

If this is the case, it is important to do a more thorough job of exploring the true root causes of the recurring problem. Gather a diverse group of affected employees and uncover trends or patterns of behavior that may indicate causes and possible solutions. Some organizations choose to include customers or people with completely different perspectives to come in with "fresh eyes" and review the situation. Study the customers' "moments of truth" with corresponding integrity matrixes, and the real problem and solution will become apparent.

One additional insight from this model is to think of it beyond the external customer and consider it in terms of your internal customer (employee). Empathizing is a nonnegotiable. Fixing the problem is only a baseline response. Pulling out the red carpet is a nice, albeit needed gesture when you make a big mistake, but only serves to dig you out of a hole that you dug yourself. What will set you apart to your employees is when you model the behavior of being a hero when you don't have to be. If you show that you care enough to help them even when you aren't obligated to, you will gain employee loyalty that you may need to call upon when times get tough. Never dismiss the power of providing service recovery internally as well as externally.

Summing Up

Service recovery and service netting are not easy concepts, but they are where the "real world" meets "world class." Great organizations succeed when they consider the entire experience from customers' perspectives and implement proven solutions that align with their core vision and values.

It all comes down to this: The magic behind world-class businesses isn't some wand or magic dust but the consistent efforts of your employees to create loyal customers day in and day out.

Chapter 19

Tips for Leading Implementation

A final question remains: How do you take this unifying World Class Excellence Model and bring it to life, as renowned businesses have done?

Most organizations don't have the luxury of creating a company from the ground up with these world-class solutions already in place. Typically, these valuable insights are discovered in the process of running and growing their business.

Regardless of where you are right now—with respect to your position within your company or its phase of development—the best thing to do is start now. There's a saying: "The best time to plant a tree is 10 years ago. The second-best time to plant a tree is today." Doing whatever you can right now always put you in a better position than waiting. Your industry is crowded with people who have a plan but have never executed that plan. Your first step is to actually take action. But the question remains: What is the *right* action?

There are two keys that world-class organizations follow for any transition to be truly successful in the long term: role-modeling behaviors that are aligned with your core values and vision, and involving employees in creating the results.

How should this action roll out? Obviously, every situation is different and requires different specifics, but overall, there is a general approach that consistently gets results for world-class organizations:

+ Tackle first things first.
+ Gain alignment.
+ Model leadership.
+ Engage employees.
+ Provide world-class service.
+ Deliver operational results.

Let's look briefly at each aspect of this approach.

Tackling First Things First

The biggest mistake most people make when attempting to fix a business is to immediately start implementing some off-the-shelf system that changes everything. This "wipe the slate clean" approach became popular after the publication of Michael Hammer and James Champy's best-selling book *Reengineering the Corporation* in 1993. Unfortunately, this is an incorrect application of their work and, in the process, "throws the baby out with the bathwater." The natural consequences of this doomed approach are typically the following:

+ Massive disruption of the operation and culture, undermining productivity.
+ Stopping effective practices and undermining passion/morale.
+ Employees have feelings of confusion and betrayal.
+ Undermining the customer experience via new/unproven practices, unsure employees, unfamiliar new processes.
+ A lack of legitimate buy-in/support by employees.
+ A "program of the month" cycle is reinforced when an unsustainable new program fails within a year.

Understanding the organizational dynamics and involving the team in creating the new approach requires a particular sequence of events. The first step is to assess (without falling victim to the dreaded "analysis paralysis" problem) and develop the relationships that are necessary to achieve the ongoing results you desire. The next step is to explore, engage, listen, and learn.

Explore

Get out of the office and into the workplace operation. Your responsibility is to discover the truth about your operation: your culture and your brand. This will never happen in an office or through reports. Presentations and reports can be very helpful in identifying trends and patterns, but to apply relevant meaning to those numbers requires context. What is the purpose for the numbers? It is to track the experience and the end result of your business' products and services.

Getting out among the employees keeps you from being "handled" and allows you to connect the dots between the theory and reality of your business. Making unscheduled visits, meeting with employees involved with all facets of the work, encouraging the use of anonymous feedback and suggestions, and responding appropriately are all critical in gathering real-world information. No one—and no organization—is more vulnerable than one that is out of direct touch with their business reality.

Engage

Part of the purpose of exploring is to engage your team. Not only is this an opportunity to gather information about what is really going on in the workplace, but it is also a chance to grow your relationship with each and every team member. The foundation of any lasting organization is the trust, shared passion, and commitment to the goal and the well-being of the team. Jacob Schneid (2009) of the Momentum Group states that "employee engagement is what prompts an employee to go above and beyond job expectations. It is largely built up, and also undone, through the intense, day-to-day interaction between employees and their direct managers." Connecting with your team helps to establish the mutual respect and interdependence needed to optimize your collective potential.

Listen

Often, during times of organizational stress, leaders tend to rely more on telling rather than really communicating. Record books are overflowing with examples of failed companies whose leaders thought they had buy-in, when only to find, afterward, that employees were simply "doing as they were told." The only difference between a choice and an informed choice is the information. Having the attitude that you already know everything that needs to be known to make a decision is a dangerous position.

As stated in discussing the five essential customer needs in chapter 2, in relation to the Customer Compass, people need to feel understood, to contribute, and to feel significant—all three aspects of engaging them for their opinions and ideas. To accomplish this, we need to do a much better job of really listening to their words and the meaning of those words.

Learn

Paying attention during this process and remaining focused on the purpose of beginning this transformative effort results in learning what could possibly bridge the gap between where you are and where you want to be. Growing as a person—or a business—is impossible without learning. This process also models behavior for the rest of the team—exhibiting how important it is to continuously learn and reinforce the process of engaging different perspectives and to what end.

Gaining Alignment

While you are in the process of gathering information and engaging the team, the next most significant action to take is to identify the company's core vision and values. As covered in part I, the process of aligning all your organization's decisions and behaviors with your core values and vision is what creates clarity, efficiencies, consistency, and, ultimately, the integrity that leads to success. Identifying the components that define the heart and soul of the organization provides a clear target toward which everyone can focus all improvement efforts.

For the handful of companies that are starting out or need to do a complete overhaul of their operations, this is the point at which you would need to gather the people who are the strategic visionaries, the star employees, and the passionate stakeholders to develop these core elements to provide tools to optimize your results. Most companies, however, already have established values and a vision (as well as core competencies, target markets, and the like). For these organizations, the goals are to

✦ Review what you have and change where needed.

✦ Better utilize your existing core as an operational success tool.

The next step of the process is announcing initiative/effort and the goal of transforming the operation. At this point, it isn't necessary to share a lot of detailed data. The goals for this step are to communicate:

✦ The way business has been conducted is no longer good enough.

✦ The company will be refocusing on the core that everyone desires.

✦ This is not a program but an ongoing process and way of thinking.

✦ We will share process and structure, but we will all create the details.

✦ Everyone is expected to be involved in sharing the best ideas about how to accomplish goals.

✦ How we achieve our goals is just as important as the goals themselves.

✦ It will be a challenge, but working together, we can be successful.

✦ You have every faith in your team.

Modeling Leadership

Once the core has been identified, the next decisive step is to ensure that leaders throughout the organization (not just those with titles or direct reports) are modeling the behaviors that reflect the core vision and values. Everything becomes more intense during times of change. What employees need during this challenging phase is

✦ a connection to the goals of the company

✦ faith in the transformation process

✦ trust in their leaders.

When things change, by definition, the "rules" for success also need to change. People have an instinctive need for some measure of stability during this unstable time. What is the employee's litmus test for the initiative? It's the organization's leaders—both formal and informal.

The employee's thought process tends to be the following: "The leaders are attending these closed-door meetings and know far more about what's really going on around here than I do. If this initiative is really legitimate, then they will be passionate about doing the behaviors they say are important." It is human nature to hear the words but pay attention to the actions. Every word, every nonverbal gesture, the way the leaders spend their time and budget—all define what each employee considers the truth about the situation.

Not only is this a critical time for leaders to encourage employees with their appropriate confidence, but their behaviors must also begin to be more closely aligned with your core—because that is to become the backbone of the organization. Drawing people to the core is what unifies the team. Basing decisions with an "investment mentality" on the core generates confidence and models good judgment. Making an effort to build relationships and trust provides an example for all employees. Initiating open and honest communication sets the foundation for effective communication as a way of doing business. This creates an environment within which the employees are engaged and delivering consistent excellent results.

Engaging Employees

The key to world-class results is a world-class organizational culture. The culture is what employees habitually do and say. The personality of your business is largely based on your employees and how much they support bringing your core vision and values to life.

Employee engagement is the catalyst that sparks passion to accomplish your corporate goals. There is a direct correlation between the amount of relevant involvement and the degree of buy-in and ownership an employee has for the company initiative. The internal processes that engage employees include

+ Providing equal opportunities for significant input.
+ Discerning opportunities to influence and to be successful.

✦ Establishing team dynamics that support the designed culture.

✦ Recognition for their properly aligned efforts.

Begin by gathering employees together in small groups to identify the things they think could improve the results of the company's efforts. Document what they suggest to make it easier to work together most effectively across all functions, consistently exceed the expectations of the customers, and generate optimal returns on every investment made by the company. One way to do this is the "stop, continue, start" process. Ask everyone:

✦ What should the organization stop doing that it is currently doing?

✦ What should the organization continue to do that is working well?

✦ What should the organization start doing that it is not currently doing?

Once this information has been documented, employees can then take ownership of creating action plans to resolve whatever issues they identify, based on priorities established by the company (the core vision and values, the Customer Compass, and current industry business challenges).

Consistently engaging employees in an ongoing conversation about these issues will create a culture of empowerment, collaboration, and unity. There is a saying: "Those who plan the fight won't fight the plan." When employees understand and design the solution, they rarely, if ever, resist supporting its implementation.

Providing World-Class Service

Once systems have been improved internally, you will have the requisite infrastructure to make an impact on external service. Leadership is modeling behavior and employees are participating in developing a culture of excellence—all with a focus on delivering an extraordinary experience to their customers. Because the branded service behaviors have been modeled internally, it becomes clear what behaviors are expected with external customers.

Employees are encouraged to engage customers as they themselves have been engaged. Interactions, rather than mere transactions, establish relationships that enhance loyalty and access feedback that can be used to continue to improve the company's effectiveness. Reinforce success stories by acknowledging:

+ the circumstances
+ the behaviors
+ the result for the customer's experience
+ the connection of the behaviors to the core vision and values
+ the impact these behaviors and the ultimate experience have on the company's reputation and brand
+ the benefit this success has for everyone in the organization.

After this, reinforce the expectation that everyone deliver behaviors and results like the success story example, and then explore new low-cost or no-cost ways to replicate that success. Consistently exceeding your customers' expectations will have a positive effect on customer satisfaction levels as well as on repeat visits, referrals, and the revenue generated by the work team.

Delivering Operational Results

Keeping track of progress is fundamental to being responsible with the organization's resources. It is vital to assess what are the most effective measurements to serve as a tool for ongoing continuous improvement. Part of becoming world class is letting go of unnecessary measurement efforts and identifying the most relevant aspects of your operations.

Numerous quantitative and qualitative measures are driven by your industry and your unique operations. These provide important details that eventually coalesce to support three primary questions:

+ To the employee: How likely is it that you would refer your family and friends to work here?
+ To the customer: How likely is it that you would refer your family and friends do business here?
+ Regarding operations: How well do our investments optimize our sustainable profit margins and grow our business?

Involve the front line—not only in identifying improvement opportunities but also in measuring the continuous improvement process. Share the details of the budget, and all the other details with which leaders are provided, when making decisions about the investment of money, effort, and time. Ensuring that employees have all the access to information they need will allow them to use their best judgment in every situation.

Generate synergy among all functional units by hosting "trade show"–like internal events to showcase the best results—with prizes awarded to those who excel in important categories (aligned with your core, of course).

Ultimately, the goal is "to be better today than we were yesterday," using the core as your North Star. If this is fully modeled and supported throughout the organization, then this initiative will never go out of style. World-class companies adopt this approach as more than a process; it is a way of thinking that has proven to be the most effective way to do business.

Chapter 20

Leading Forward to World-Class Excellence

Although we have reviewed strategies and tactics for you to move your organization forward and achieve world-class excellence, we haven't yet addressed what you need as a leader to start this journey. As we mentioned at the opening of this book, though your organization is similar to others with regard to the comprehensive World Class Excellence Model, your organization is also completely unique in its culture and industry challenges. Your successful implementation will rely, first, on your exercise of leadership. In chapter 1, we described the Chain Reaction of Excellence Model, which we show again here, in figure 20-1.

The focus of this book has been on putting your customers—internal and external—first and thus creating a culture of excellence for your employees while building a brand with highly satisfied and loyal customers. In

Figure 20-1. The Chain Reaction of Excellence Model

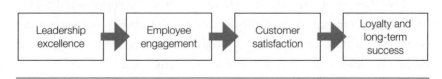

these last few pages, we return to our discussion of leadership excellence and what it will take for you to implement these best-in-business ideas in your own organization.

Take Courage

One of the most critical leadership traits for moving an organization forward is courage. "Courage" comes from the French word *coeur*, which means to have heart. The heart is a common symbol of inner strength. So courage means to have the heart, the inner strength, and/or the will to do something. We draw courage from what we believe in, what we value, what we love. The level of courage we bring to a situation will be in proportion to how strongly we believe in the purpose of the situation. Courage, therefore, is defined as "choosing to act in the face of fear for a purpose."

We best apply courage when we directly face our concerns and fears. "Fear" seems like a strong word. We usually associate it with a life-and-death situation. For our purposes, the definition of fear is "a distressing emotion around an impending concern, apprehension, or dismay." Most fears relate to uncertainties or doubts that we may experience.

In the real world, what challenges or fears do people typically face when they try to implement the kinds of best-in-business ideas we have been describing? People think things such as

+ No one else will get on board or take ownership.
+ Budget cuts will prevent us from doing anything meaningful.
+ Those at the top just don't get it.
+ We're in the middle of so much organizational change that no one can focus on this.
+ It will just end up as another temporary initiative.

Call these concerns or call them fears, but in the end you must have the will to overcome them. How do you get this will? By focusing more on your goal than your obstacle. What is really needed to bring about change is choosing to act more on what we value than what we fear.

And what do we value? Look back at the content of part I of this book. The driving force—the catalyst and fuel for action—rests in an organization's core vision and values. Average organizations may treat values like things that are nice to have, but world-class organizations are energized by their values. They live and breathe these core truths and, in doing so, they stand apart as different from and better than their competitors. And by embodying their values, they create a compelling vision for how to move forward. Ambrose Redmoon said it well: "Courage is not the absence of fear, but rather the judgment that something else is more important than fear."

Too often, we think that we will try to implement the kinds of ideas described in this book when things "get better." The truth is, taking action itself is what *makes* things better. Waiting for "better" only makes things worse. Your role is to take courage and act now—despite the fact that your situation is less than ideal. Courage is best applied when you act on what you can control (your behaviors) and/or influence (your surroundings).

Choose to Act

The greatest power that a person possesses is the power to choose.
—J. Martin Kohe

We stated above that courage was "choosing to act in the face of fear for a purpose." "I choose" is one of the most powerful statements you can make to demonstrate ownership. Similarly, "We choose" is one of the most powerful statements a team can make. It is a statement of ownership and accountability, as well as courage, when we choose to implement new ways of doing things—even in the face of fears related to our own job security or personal ability to adapt—and are willing to be held accountable for the consequences.

We encourage you to choose. Choose to do *something.* Choose to exercise influence. Choose to walk in the shoes of others. Choose to understand others' needs, others' expectations, others' individual styles. Choose to respond to something you value most. Choose to follow a vision that will drive your organization toward excellence. Choose to create truly outstanding service. Choose to engage your fellow employees.

Choose daily and constantly, and in the little things. Choose to do some little act today to start. Choose to do something each and every day to make a difference. Choose to make a habit of being excellent each and every day.

You really can be world class. You only need to choose—and take action.

Choose. Act. Succeed. Today.

We are what we repeatedly do.
Excellence, therefore, is not an act, but a habit.
—Aristotle

References

Barber, Allison. 2009. Interview with the vice president of talent management for Starwood Hotels & Resorts by one of the authors, December.

Barlow, Janelle, and Paul Stewart. 2004. *Branded Customer Service: The New Competitive Edge.* San Francisco: Berrett-Koehler.

Barrett, Colleen. 2008. Talking Southwest Culture. *Spirit Magazine,* May.

Berkun, Scott. 2005. How to Learn from Your Mistakes. Essay 44. July 17. http://www.scottberkun.com/essays/44-how-to-learn-from-your-mistakes/.

Clark, Margaret M. 2004. A Jury of Their Peers: Giving Employees a Say in Resolving Each Other's Workplace Disputes Can Pay Big Cultural Dividends—Employee Relations. *HR Magazine,* January. http://findarticles.com/p/articles/mi_m3495/is_1_49/ai_112799813.

Cockerell, Lee. 2008. *Creating Magic: 10 Common Sense Leadership Strategies from a Life at Disney.* New York: Doubleday.

Cohen, David S. 2006. *Inside the Box: Leading with Corporate Values to Drive Sustained Business Success.* New York: John Wiley & Sons.

Consumer Reports. 2008. Toyota and Honda Top Automotive Brands in Consumer Perception. January. http://www.consumerreports.org/cro/cars/new-cars/news/2008/01/brand-perceptions/overview/brand-perceptions-top-5.htm.

Covey, Stephen R. 1989. *The 7 Habits of Highly Effective People.* New York: Simon & Schuster.

DeSantiago, Michael F. 2009. Author interview with president of Primera Engineering Ltd. August.

Eyring, Pam. 2009. Interview with the president of the Protocol School of Washington by one of the authors, December.

Fortune. 2008. 100 Best Companies to Work For: 74—Granite Construction and 100 Best Companies to Work For: 82—Nike. http://money.cnn.com/magazines/fortune/bestcompanies/2008.

Fortune. 2007. America's Most Admired Companies, Apple: America's Best Retailer. March 8. http://money.cnn.com.

Gallup Consulting. 2009. Employee Engagement: A Leading Indicator of Financial Performance. December 17. http://www.gallup.com/consulting/52/employee-engagement.aspx.

Gardner, Joseph. 2009. Interview with the director of leadership at the Gaylord National Hotel by one of the authors, September.

Hammer, Michael, and James Champy. 1993. *Reengineering the Corporation: A Manifesto for Business Revolution.* New York: HarperCollins.

Harvard Business Review. 1997. Ideas at Work. January–February.

Hawn, Carleen. 2008. Brad Bird on Fostering Innovation. *Gigaom.com,* April 17.

Jargon, Julie. 2009. Latest Starbucks Buzzword: Lean Japanese Techniques. *Wall Street Journal Online,* August 4. http://online.wsj.com/article/SB124933474023402611.html.

Kliff, Matthew. 2008. Author interview with manager of inflight training, Jet Blue University. December.

Kober, J. Jeff. 2009. *The Wonderful World of Customer Service at Disney.* Kissimmee, FL: Performance Journeys Publishing.

Kotter, John, and James Heskett. 1992. *Corporate Culture and Performance.* New York: Simon & Schuster.

Lofy, Chuck, and Mary M. Lofy. 2003. *Vitality: Igniting Your Organization's Spirit.* Menlo Park, CA: Crisp Learning.

Lorber, Laura. 2008. Giving Employees a Say in Where They'll Work. *WSJ .com/Small Business,* January 17. http://www.smsmallbiz.com/bestpractices/Giving_Employees_a_Say_in_Where_They_Will_Work.html.

Marriott, Richard E. 2003. Building a Family Legacy: The Marriott Story. *Marriott Magazine,* Winter, 4–7. http://marriottschool.byu.edu/the-marriott -story.pdf.

McGraw, Mark. 2008. Containing Healthcare Costs. *Human Resource Executive Online,* October 22. http://www.hrexecutive.com/HRE/story.jsp?storyId =139625418.

MetLife. 2007. *Fifth Annual Study of Employee Benefits Trends: Findings from the National Survey of Employers and Employees.* New York: MetLife. https://broker.beerepurves.com/News/Newsletter/pdf/Apr2007/MetLifeEBTS .pdf.

Michelli, Joseph A. 2008. *The New Gold Standard: 5 Leadership Principles for Creating a Legendary Customer Service Experience Courtesy of the Ritz-Carlton Hotel Company.* New York: McGraw-Hill.

Millard, Nicole J. 2009. Author interview with the customer experience futur-ologist for BT. March.

Mills, Elinor. 2007. Meet Google's Culture Czar. *ZDNet*, April 30.

Nelson, Bill. 2002. Get the Most from Your Mistakes. *Washington Business Journal*, November 1.

Norberg, Elizabeth. 2009. Author interview with senior vice president of human resources for Dolce Hotels and Resorts. December.

Peters, Thomas J., and Robert H. Waterman. 1984. *In Search of Excellence: Lessons from America's Best-Run Companies.* New York: HarperCollins.

Pine, Joseph, II, and James H. Gilmore. 1999. *The Experience Economy: Work Is Theatre & Every Business a Stage.* Boston: Harvard Business Press.

Pyke, Bob. 2009. iPods to Educate Bariactric Patients. Nursing Informatics Online, http://www.informaticsnurse.com.

Reichheld, Frederick F. 2001. *The Loyalty Effect: The Hidden Force behind Growth, Profits, and Lasting Value.* Boston: Harvard Business Publishing.

Reid, Roger H., and David W. Merrill. 1981. *Personal Styles & Effective Performance.* New York: CRC Press.

Robert Wood Johnson Foundation. 2008. Reducing Anxiety and Increasing Patient-Centeredness with a Welcome Video. June 4. http://www.rwjf .org/qualityequality/product.jsp?id=30272.

Robinson, Jeremy. 2010. Author interview with director of human resources at Florida Hospital Celebration Health.

Sanborn, Mark. 2008. *The Encore Effect: How to Achieve Remarkable Performance in Anything You Do.* Colorado Springs: Waterbrook Press.

Scarbrough, Shelby. 2009. Author interview with past president of Entrepre-neurs Organization. November.

Schneid, Jacob. 2009. Employee Engagement: You Have to Get Up Close and Personal. Unpublished manuscript.

Stoller, Gary. 2005. Companies Give Front-Line Employees More Power. *USA Today.* June 26.

Thomas, Bob. 1998. *Building a Company: Roy O. Disney and the Creation of an Enter-tainment Empire.* New York: Hyperion.

Tudor, Kim. 2009. Author interview with the director of the Barbados National Initiative for Service Excellence. March.

Underhill, Paco. 2000. *Why We Buy: The Science of Shopping.* New York: Simon & Schuster.

About the Authors

 **Mark David Jones** is Chief Operating Officer of World Class Benchmarking. During the past two decades, he has been a consultant to dozens of *Fortune* 500 companies around the world. As an author and highly demanded speaker, he is known for his innovative, results-focused passion.

Mark's career at the Walt Disney Company spanned 26 years, working in a wide variety of leadership roles throughout Operations, Guest Relations, and Human Resources—spearheading executive development and organizational change efforts. While serving as the Senior Consultant for the Disney Institute, Mark was in charge of leadership, creativity and innovation, and quality service initiatives. In recognition of his contribution to the Disney organization, Mark was nominated for the prestigious Partners in Excellence award—Disney's highest regarded corporate award.

J. Jeff Kober is Chief Executive Officer of World Class Benchmarking. For over 25 years, Jeff has provided training and development solutions for workplaces around the world. Beyond his many keynotes and seminars, he has worked as a consultant with scores of organizations in the private and public sector to improve the work of employees and leaders alike.

A former leader of the Disney Institute, Jeff collaborated across the entire Walt Disney World organization in establishing customer service and creativity programming. Since then he has become an online columnist on Disney benchmarking practices and creator of the "Disney at Work" app tour series for the iPhone. He is the author of *The Wonderful World of Customer Service at Disney* and is considered the foremost thought leader on best-in-business practices in the Walt Disney Company.

About World Class Benchmarking

World Class Benchmarking was created from a passion to help professionals like you bridge the gap between conceptual business strategy and successful tactical implementation. After accomplished careers leading public and private sector organizations, Jeff Kober and Mark David Jones met while developing the Disney Institute—where business people from all over the world come to learn how the Disney Corporation was so wildly successful. Jeff and Mark were responsible for designing and implementing the business content for the institute that reveals the operational tactics needed to create customer and employee "magic." After years of working with Disney as well as dozens of *Fortune* 100 companies, Jeff and Mark noticed a striking pattern: the world's most renowned organizations, regardless of industry, followed the same approach to sustained excellence. As their reputation for successful organizational transformation grew, leaders from other world-class organizations encouraged Jeff and Mark to share the "behind the scenes" insights from their relationships with the best-of-the-best corporations around the world. In early 2005, they launched World Class Benchmarking, Inc. to share the proven approach to success through on-site business management consulting and their open-enrollment best-practice programs in Orlando, Florida, and other major cities.

Today, Jeff and Mark are thrilled to continue helping businesses, employees, customers, and worldwide communities realize their potential each day. The next success could be yours! Contact World Class Benchmarking today online at www.WorldClassBenchmarking.com or call toll-free: 1-877-4 WCB NOW.

Index